The Big Book of Holidays and Cultural Celebrations

Author

Suzanne Barchers

SHELL EDUCATION

Credits

Publishing Credits

Robin Erickson, *Production Director;* Lee Aucoin, *Creative Director;*
Timothy J. Bradley, *Illustration Manager;* Sara Johnson, M.S.Ed., *Editorial Director;*
Jennifer Viñas, *Editor;* Grace Alba, *Designer;* Stephanie Reid, *Photo Editor;*
Aly Armour, *Creative Assistant;* Amber Goff, *Creative Assistant;*
Corinne Burton, M.A.Ed., *Publisher*

Image Credits

pp.119–127, p.223, p.279, p.287 Clip Art; p.20, p.69, p.71, p.80, p.167, p.171, p.282 Dreamstime; p.8, p.12, p.26, p.28, pp. 34–59, pp.68–76, p.96, pp.98–99, pp.103–110, p.115, pp.130–131, pp.147–149, p.154–161, pp. 168, p.171, pp.182–183, p.214, p.222, p.228, p.239, p.246, p.266, pp.277–280, p.286 iStock; p.16, p.24, pp.32–33, p.42-43, p.51, p.59, p.67, pp.75–76, pp.84–85, pp.93–94, p.102, p.118, pp.126–127, pp.135–136, pp.144, pp.152–153, p.161, p.169, pp.177–178, p.186, p.194, p.202, p.210, p.218, p.226, pp.234–235, p.243, p.251–252, pp.260–261, pp.269–270 Stephanie Reid; p.110 Hillary Dunlap; all other images Shutterstock

---

Shell Education

5301 Oceanus Drive
Huntington Beach, CA 92649-1030
http://www.shelleducation.com
ISBN 978-1-4258-1046-7
©2014 Shell Educational Publishing, Inc.

Table of Contents

Introduction

Did you know...

- That wearing new clothes on Easter is considered lucky?

- That Punxsutawney Phil has been around since 1886? His predecessors date back to ancient Roman times when a badger or a hedgehog predicted whether a second winter would follow during a festival called Candlemas.

- That in the 18th and 19th centuries, British children went door to door asking for treats on Valentine's Day?

- That Cinco de Mayo celebrates a day when a greatly outnumbered ragtag Mexican army won a battle against troops sent by Napoleon III?

- That Decoration Day is the official name of Memorial Day?

- That Independence Day was first celebrated in Philadelphia in 1777?

- That the shofar, used during Rosh Hashanah, is made from a ram's horn?

- That *Diwali* means *row of lamps* in Sanskrit?

- That April Fools' Day may date back to the time when Charles IX adopted the Gregorian Calendar? New Year's Day was moved from the end of March to January 1, and it took a while for everyone to learn about the change. Those who celebrated on April 1 were called April Fools.

For thousands of years, people have recognized or celebrated significant points in time. Some ancient societies celebrated the New Year in the fall when the harvest was complete. Some cultures celebrated New Year with the arrival of spring, seen as a time of the Earth's renewal. Once calendars were adopted, celebrations became more formal. Celtic tribes celebrated the Sun God and the Lord of the Dead, Samhain, on November 1. In late December, the Romans celebrated Saturnalia, honoring the Golden Age of Saturn, the god of sowing and husbandry. Many cultures celebrated with similar features, such as those observances that used sources of light such as candles, lanterns, or bonfires.

Although there are 10 federal holidays in the United States, there are many other important days throughout the year that carry religious, historical, family, or whimsical significance. *The Big Book of Holidays and Cultural Celebrations K–2* provides the opportunity to celebrate and learn about more than 30 of those special times.

About This Book

Teachers and students who use *The Big Book of Holidays and Cultural Celebrations K–2* will benefit from various factors.

Connecting to Various Cultures

Students in our classrooms come from increasingly diverse backgrounds. *The Big Book of Holidays and Cultural Celebrations K–2* provides resources for the most commonly celebrated holidays, special days, and religious events. Your classroom may have just one student who celebrates a particular festival or religious observance. However, the classroom that explores this and other cultural celebrations will discover universal themes (New Year's Day celebrations), parallels (the many celebrations that use lights or special foods), and practices that are intriguing (Groundhog Day) or simply fun (trick-or-treating).

Connecting to History

Americans have always freely adopted elements from other cultures, often without even knowing why. After all, you don't have to be Irish or know much about the patron saint of Ireland to enjoy wearing a bit of green on St. Patrick's Day. But knowing about Saint Patrick's life and why the first United States parades were held in the 1700s enriches the experience. People may recognize the importance of honoring our veterans without realizing that November 11 originally honored the armistice signed that day in 1918, ending World War I—on the 11th hour of the 11th day of the 11th month. The story of Passover, which recounts the exodus of the enslaved Jews, has resonated with African Americans for hundreds of years and given voice with the plea of *Let my people go*. Although not a history or social studies curriculum, the content in this resource provides context for discussion, with additional information provided on how some celebrations are still observed around the world.

Enhancing and Developing Skills

Through the activities in this *book*, students will explore important academic skills, such as using meaning clues and mental images to aid comprehension. The variety of choices for each holiday provides for differentiation, allowing you to select activities appropriate for individuals or groups of students. The activities build on and develop the following:

- Critical-thinking skills
- Creative-thinking skills
- Vocabulary skills
- Reading skills
- Spelling skills
- Math skills

Engaging Learners

During times of exciting holidays, such as Halloween or Valentine's Day, it can be challenging to keep young students focused. The activities in *Holidays and Cultural Celebrations* provide teachers and students with activities that will give some context to the holiday while keeping the students fully engaged.

How to Use This Book

Each observance has one page of background information for the teacher and seven pages of activities. The activity sheets, which vary from unit to unit, are designed for independent work. For younger students or those with special needs, you may want to help with directions or background information. However, once students have used a number of the activities, they will readily understand the purpose in subsequent units.

Background Information

This page gives you details about the observance. It provides the context for the choices made in the activity pages. You may want to share some of the information with the students before using some of the activity sheets. This page also includes a list of recommended books and information about places in the world where the observance occurs.

Riddles

This activity uses a riddle format to provide information about key words and concepts. The Word Bank allows students to make thoughtful choices whether they have relevant background knowledge or do not.

Mixed-Up Words

This word-scramble activity allows students to combine decoding skills with picture reading while practicing their spelling skills.

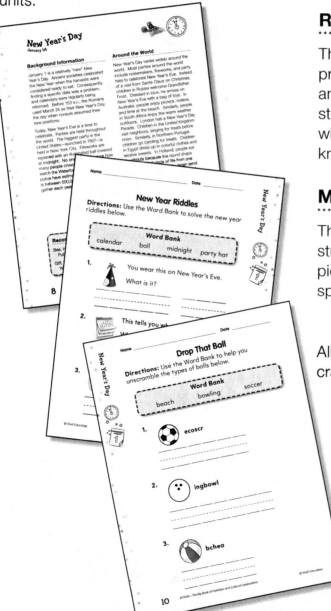

All of the activity pages and pictures of crafts are on the **Digital Resource CD**.

How to Use This Book (cont.)

Connect the Words

This activity provides practice with multisyllabic, compound, or two-word phrases, reinforcing word analysis skills.

Word Search

This activity provides students with practice finding key vocabulary words. In some instances, students build a sentence from the relevant words.

Maze

This activity allows students to think ahead so that they make it through the correct path.

Look Again!

This activity allows students to examine an image for differences.

Writing

Some activities include writing, such as writing acrostic poems, writing messages, alphabetizating, and wordplay.

Craft Activity

Each unit includes at least one craft activity. These use routinely available materials. Many of the art processes can be applied to other projects.

Reader's Theater

Many of the observances end with a choral reading. You may determine that using this at the beginning of a unit helps provide the background information for completion of the activity sheets. In other instances, the choral reading can be used for a holiday program for families or other classes. The script can also serve as a culminating activity for a more in-depth exploration of a theme, such as a study of Abraham Lincoln and George Washington. Feel free to copy the script and adjust the character assignments for small-group readings.

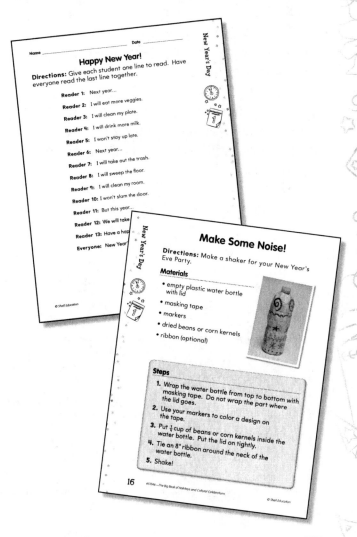

New Year's Day
January 1st

Background Information

January 1 is a relatively "new" New Year's Day. Ancient societies celebrated the New Year when the harvests were considered ready to eat. Consequently, finding a specific date was a problem, and calendars were regularly being reformed. Before 153 B.C., the Romans used March 24 as their New Year's Day, the day when consuls assumed their new positions.

Today, New Year's Eve is a time to celebrate. Parties are held throughout the world. The biggest party in the United States—launched in 1907—is held in New York City. Fireworks are replaced with an illuminated ball lowered at midnight. No one knows for sure how many people crowd into Times Square to watch the Waterford crystal ball drop, but police have estimated in the past that it is between 500,000 and a million people gather each year.

Around the World

New Year's Day varies widely around the world. Most parties around the world include noisemakers, fireworks, and party hats to celebrate New Year's Eve. Instead of a visit from Santa Claus on Christmas, children in Russia welcome Grandfather Frost. Dressed in blue, he arrives on New Year's Eve with a bag of toys. In Australia, people enjoy picnics, rodeos, and time at the beach. Similarly, people in South Africa enjoy the warm weather outdoors. London has a New Year's Day Parade. Children in the United Kingdom visit neighbors, singing for treats before noon. Similarly, in Northern Portugal, children go caroling for treats. Children in Egypt dress up in colorful clothes and receive sweets. In Holland, people eat doughnuts because the round shape stands for a full circle of life from one year to the next. People in Japan send postcards to friends and family so that they arrive on January 1, and children receive gifts of money. People in Korea visit their families and play traditional games. Even though New Year's Day is celebrated in different ways, people from all over the world get excited for the new year ahead.

Recommended Books

Bae, Hyun-Joo. 2007. *New Clothes for New Year's Day*. LaJolla, CA: Kane/Miller Publishing.

Giff, Patricia Reilly. 1990. *Emily Arrow Promises to Do Better This Year*. New York: Yearling.

Name _____   **Date** _____

New Year Riddles

Directions: Use the Word Bank to solve the new year riddles below.

Word Bank

calendar   ball   midnight   party hat

1. You wear this on New Year's Eve.

What is it?

_____ _____ _____ _____   _____ _____ _____

-     - - - - - - - - - - - - -

_____ _____ _____ _____   _____ _____ _____

2.  This tells you what day it is.

What is it?

_____ _____ _____ _____ _____ _____ _____ _____

- -

_____ _____ _____ _____ _____ _____ _____ _____

3. This is the time the new year starts.

What time is it?

_____ _____ _____ _____ _____ _____ _____ _____

- -

_____ _____ _____ _____ _____ _____ _____ _____

Name _____   Date _____

Drop That Ball

Directions: Use the Word Bank to help you unscramble the types of balls below.

Word Bank

beach   bowling   soccer

---

1.      **ecoscr**

___ ___ ___ ___ ___ ___

- - - - - - - - - - - - - - - - - - - -

___ ___ ___ ___ ___ ___

2.      **ingbowl**

___ ___ ___ ___ ___ ___ ___

- - - - - - - - - - - - - - - - - - - -

___ ___ ___ ___ ___ ___ ___

3.   **bchea**

___ ___ ___ ___ ___

- - - - - - - - - - - - - - - - - - - -

___ ___ ___ ___ ___

Connect the Party Hats

Directions: Match each addition problem on the left to its answer on the right.

4 + 3 =

2 + 7 =

10 + 5 =

8 + 4 =

9 + 2 =

9

7

15

11

12

Name _____   Date _____

Connect the New Year's Words

Directions: Draw a line to match the New Year's word parts. Use the pictures to help you.

noise

night

mid

maker

calen

dar

ba

corn

pop

by

#51046—*The Big Book of Holidays and Cultural Celebrations*

Name _____ Date _____

My New Year's Resolutions

Directions: Think about what you want to do for the new year. Cut and paste the New Year's resolutions below onto the calendar (page 14) in the months you would like to focus on doing them really well. Of course you may wish to do them all year long!

read more books

eat healthy breakfasts

brush teeth more

wear a bike helmet

wear sunscreen

eat more vegetables

help clean the house

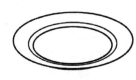

help clean the dishes

play with my pet more

be kinder to others

work harder at school

exercise more

Name _____ Date _____

My New Year's Resolutions (cont.)

January	February	March
April	**May**	**June**
July	**August**	**September**
October	**November**	**December**

#51046—The Big Book of Holidays and Cultural Celebrations   © Shell Education

Name _____   Date _____

Happy New Year!

Directions: Give each student one line to read. Have everyone read the last line together.

Reader 1: Next year...

Reader 2: I will eat more veggies.

Reader 3: I will clean my plate.

Reader 4: I will drink more milk.

Reader 5: I won't stay up late.

Reader 6: Next year...

Reader 7: I will take out the trash.

Reader 8: I will sweep the floor.

Reader 9: I will clean my room.

Reader 10: I won't slam the door.

Reader 11: But this year...

Reader 12: We will take the time to say...

Reader 13: Have a happy...

Everyone: New Year's Day!

Make Some Noise!

Directions: Make a shaker for your New Year's Eve Party.

Materials

- empty plastic water bottle with lid
- masking tape
- markers
- dried beans or corn kernels
- ribbon (optional)

Steps

1. Wrap the water bottle from top to bottom with masking tape. Do not wrap the part where the lid goes.

2. Use your markers to color a design on the tape.

3. Put $\frac{1}{4}$ cup of beans or corn kernels inside the water bottle. Put the lid on tightly.

4. Tie an 8" ribbon around the neck of the water bottle.

5. Shake!

Martin Luther King Jr. Day
Third Monday of January

Background Information

Martin Luther King Jr. was born on January 15, 1929, into a family of three generations of Baptist ministers. He lived in Atlanta for his first 12 years. He attended Atlanta's Morehouse College from 1944 to 1948, where he began his journey of blending Christianity with the movement of progressive social change. He studied at Crozer Theological Seminary and completed his doctorate at Boston University's School of Theology.

During his first pastorate, at Dexter Avenue Baptist Church in Montgomery, Alabama, he became the spokesman for the yearlong Montgomery bus boycott. In 1957, he joined with other leaders to form the Southern Christian Leadership Conference, assuming the role of president.

Throughout his years of leadership, he blended his deep understanding of ideas gleaned from Mohandas Gandhi's precepts of nonviolence with those of Christian values. He was politically astute, able to bring together diverse leaders to continue the move toward improved rights for African Americans.

His accomplishments from late 1955 to his death on April 4, 1968, are unparalleled. His efforts continued beyond the desegregation laws following the Montgomery bus boycott to the Voting Rights Act in 1965. On April 3, 1968, he delivered these unforgettable words: "I've been to the mountaintop, [and] I've seen the Promised Land." He continued, "I may not get there with you. But I want you to know tonight, that we, as a people, will get to the Promised Land." The following evening, he was assassinated by James Earl Ray.

Around the World

Dr. Martin Luther King Jr. is the only person who was not a president to have a national holiday named for him. Dr. King is recognized around the world for his work as a civil-rights leader. Memorials can be seen in Sweden and England. He was the youngest person at the time to receive the Nobel Peace Prize. He worked to end apartheid in South Africa, and his efforts were continued by his wife, Coretta Scott King, after his death.

Recommended Books

Adler, David A. 1990. *A Picture Book of Martin Luther King Jr.* New York City: Holiday House.

Rappaport, Doreen. 2007. *Martin's Big Words: The Life of Dr. Martin Luther King Jr.* New York: Hyperion Book.

Ringgold, Faith. 1998. *My Dream of Martin Luther King.* New York City: Dragonfly Books.

Name _____   Date _____

Dr. King Riddles

Directions: Use the Word Bank to solve the Martin Luther King Jr. riddles below.

Word Bank

bus   church   peace   dream

1.   This is where Dr. King worked.

What is it?

___ ___ ___ ___ ___ ___

- -

___ ___ ___ ___ ___ ___

2.    Rosa Parks rode on this.

What is it?

___ ___ ___

- - - - - - - - - - - - - - - - - -

___ ___ ___

3.    Dr. King wished for this.

What is it?

___ ___ ___ ___ ___

- -

___ ___ ___ ___ ___

#51046—The Big Book of Holidays and Cultural Celebrations

Name _____   **Date** _____

Words of Peace

Directions: Use the Word Bank to help you unscramble the words below.

Word Bank

dove   friends   hands   dream

1.

endsfri   _ _ _ _ _ _ _

2.

maerd   _ _ _ _ _

3.

vedo   _ _ _ _

4.

ndsha   _ _ _ _ _

#51046—The Big Book of Holidays and Cultural Celebrations

Name _____   Date _____

Connect the Dr. King Words

Directions: Draw a line to match the words. Use the pictures to help you.

Martin Luther   **Parks**

voting   **King Jr.**

Rosa   **rights**

Nobel   **a dream**

I have   **Peace Prize**

Name _____   **Date** _____

Dr. King Word Search

Directions: Find and circle the words in the Word Bank hidden in the puzzle.

Word Bank

| church | love | dream | peace |
| vote | freedom | march | preacher |

l	o	v	e	r	l	d	i	m	c	c	c	f
t	m	r	p	c	p	r	e	a	c	h	e	r
f	e	o	m	p	i	e	c	r	p	u	s	x
v	o	t	e	t	t	a	i	c	t	r	h	e
f	r	e	e	d	o	m	o	h	l	c	t	r
t	p	e	a	c	e	f	u	h	e	h	t	o

#51046—The Big Book of Holidays and Cultural Celebrations

Connect the Doves

Directions: Match each addition problem on the left to its answer on the right.

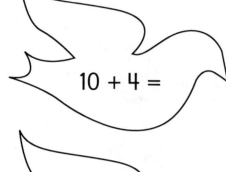

10 + 4 =

12

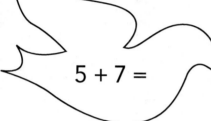

5 + 7 =

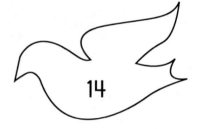

14

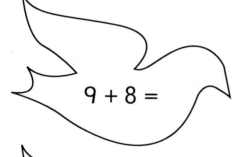

9 + 8 =

17

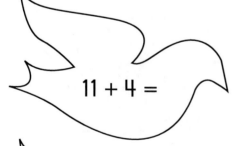

11 + 4 =

6

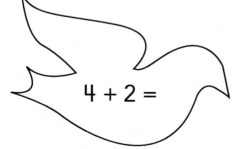

4 + 2 =

15

Name _____ Date _____

"I Have a Dream" Poem

Directions: Write an acrostic poem using words that describe Dr. Martin Luther King Jr.

M _____
_____

A _____
_____

R _____
_____

T _____
_____

I _____
_____

N _____
_____

Hands of Peace

Directions: Make a symbol of peace to honor Dr. Martin Luther King Jr.

Materials

- paper plate
- picture of Dr. King
- construction paper (various colors)
- pencil
- scissors
- glue

Steps

1. Glue the picture of Martin Luther King Jr. in the center of the paper plate.
2. Trace your hand onto a piece of construction paper.
3. Cut out the hand.
4. Place the hand on the edge of a paper plate.
5. Cut out more hands to make a border.
6. Arrange the hands in a nice pattern of colors.
7. Glue the hands in place.

Chinese New Year
Late January to Mid February

Background Information

The Chinese calendar, historically set by the emperor, represents complex mathematics and traditional symbols. Chinese New Year, also known as the Lunar New Year, is celebrated on the first day of the first month of the Chinese calendar, which is influenced by the lunar phases, solar solstices, and equinoxes. Each New Year is influenced, in turn, by one of 12 animals who competed in a race that established this order: rat, ox, tiger, rabbit, dragon, snake, horse, sheep, monkey, rooster, dog, and pig. Important elements include wood, fire, earth, metal, and water.

Chinese New Year celebrations are influenced by the Taoist religion. *Yin* and *yang* are the opposing but complementary principles that make for a harmonious world, such as male and female or life and death. The New Year is important for eliminating negative forces and spirits, using noisemakers and firecrackers to frighten them away. Homes are cleaned to ensure that the negative forces of the past are gone. Positive messages such as *good fortune* or *great wealth* are shared on small scrolls or pieces of paper. Decorations are in red (a good omen) and gold (for wealth), important celebratory colors.

The celebration lasts 15 days, with traditional activities for each of the days, such as welcoming the spirits, honoring the ancestors, and preparing for the Lantern Festival, which is held on the 15th and final night. During the Lantern Festival, riddles are displayed on lanterns in the streets. Visitors can solve the riddles and receive small gifts.

Around the World

Asian countries that celebrate Chinese New Year include China, Korea, Mongolia, Nepal, and Vietnam. All U.S. cities that have a Chinese community celebrate, too. In large cities such as San Francisco and New York City, there may be parades with floats and music. There also may be dances, street fairs, and fireworks. The most fascinating member of the parade is the great Golden Dragon, one of four Divine Creatures. (The others are the Unicorn, Phoenix, and Tortoise.) These creatures dispel bad spirits.

Recommended Books

Waters, Kate. 1991. *Lion Dancer: Ernie Wan's Chinese New Year.* New York: Scholastic.

Yu, Li Qiong. 2011. *A New Year's Reunion: A Chinese Story.* Somerville, MA: Candlewick Press.

Name _____ Date _____

Chinese New Year Riddles

Directions: Use the Word Bank to solve the Chinese New Year riddles below.

Word Bank

dragon lantern tiger parade

1. It has a long tail and breathes fire.

What is it?

_____ _____ _____ _____ _____

- - - - - - - - - - - - - - - - - - - -

_____ _____ _____ _____ _____

2. It lights up the dark.

What is it?

_____ _____ _____ _____ _____

- - - - - - - - - - - - - - - - - - - -

_____ _____ _____ _____ _____

3.  It is an animal that roars.

What is it?

_____ _____ _____ _____ _____

- - - - - - - - - - - - - - - - - - - -

_____ _____ _____ _____ _____

#51046—The Big Book of Holidays and Cultural Celebrations © Shell Education

Name _____   Date _____

Chinese Zodiac Animals

Directions: Match each Zodiac animal picture to its name.

horse

dog

snake

monkey

pig

Name _____   Date _____

Connect the Parade Words

Directions: Draw a line to match the Chinese New Year word parts. Use the pictures to help you.

danc

mer

drum

ers

dra

ger

ti

gon

lan

tern

#51046—The Big Book of Holidays and Cultural Celebrations

Name _____   Date _____

Follow the Zodiac Animal!

Directions: Start at the snake. Draw a line to connect all of the snakes. Can you get to the lantern?

Start

#51046—The Big Book of Holidays and Cultural Celebrations   **29**

Name _____ Date _____

Zodiac Search

Directions: Find and circle the words in the Word Bank hidden in the puzzle.

Word Bank

dog	horse	pig	rooster
dragon	monkey	rabbit	tiger
goat	ox	rat	snake

d	r	a	g	o	n	c	p
o	o	h	o	r	s	e	i
g	o	x	a	i	u	f	g
r	s	w	t	i	g	e	r
a	t	m	o	n	k	e	y
t	e	s	n	a	k	e	o
q	r	a	b	b	i	t	z

Name _____   Date _____

Happy Chinese New Year!

Directions: Give each student one line to read. Have everyone read the last line together.

Reader 1:   The animals were called together.

Reader 2:   All the animals were ready to race.

Reader 3:   The big day came at last.

Reader 4:   Who will win first place?

Reader 5:   The dog, goat, and dragon pushed through.

Reader 6:   The rat did something worse.

Reader 7:   He jumped ahead of ox.

Reader 8:   He crossed the finish line first.

Reader 9:   Thank you to the animals.

Reader 10: We all want to cheer!

Reader 11: Have a happy Chinese New Year.

Everyone: Have a healthy, wealthy year!

Golden Dragon

Directions: Make a dragon puppet for Chinese New Year.

Materials

- *Dragon Template* (page 33)

- construction paper (various colors)

- scissors

- pencil

- glue

- marker (optional)

Steps

1. Trace your hand onto a sheet of construction paper. Cut it out. This is your pattern.

2. Use the pattern to make five more hands on separate sheets of colored paper. Cut them out.

3. Arrange the hands as in the picture to make the dragon's body. Glue in place.

4. Cut out the dragon parts from the Dragon template. Glue onto the dragon.

5. Add eyes and a nose with a marker.

Dragon Template

Groundhog Day
February 2nd

Background Information

Brought to the United States by settlers from Germany, the tradition of determining whether there would be six more weeks of winter has become an entertaining midwinter event. The most celebrated site for observing Groundhog Day has been Punxsutawney, Pennsylvania. In 1887, the *Punxsutawney Spirit* newspaper declared that the groundhog had not seen its shadow. If the groundhog had seen its shadow, there would have been six more weeks of winter.

The following year, the first trek was made to Gobbler's Knob to look for a groundhog. Clymer H. Freas, the Spirit's editor, promoted the Punxsutawney groundhog, dubbed Punxsutawney Phil, as the official weather forecaster. Over the years, the tradition grew, with people checking in on Punxsutawney Phil via the media to see whether spring will come early.

A group of Punxsutawney residents manage other events besides checking on Punxsutawney Phil on February 2. Events include a Prognosticators Ball, a chili cook off, and woodchuck whittling.

The groundhog hibernates, with its body temperature dropping to just above freezing. A groundhog's lifespan is six to eight years. However, Phil is said to have magically stayed alive since 1886 because of the magical punch he is given every year.

Around the World

The roots of Groundhog Day date back to stories about animals waking up on specific dates near the end of winter. Early Christians celebrated Candlemas Day in Europe, the day when the clergy blessed candles and distributed them to the people. The legend says, *For as the sun shines on Candlemas Day, so far will the snow swirl until May.* The Romans added to the tradition during their conquest of what is now known as Germany. They said that if the sun shines on Candlemas, an animal such as a badger or a hedgehog would cast a shadow. Thus there would be six more weeks of bad weather, the *second winter.* The groundhog was determined to be the closest to the European badger or hedgehog.

Recommended Books

Balian, Lorna. 2011. *A Garden for a Groundhog*. Cambridge, MA: Star Bright Books.

Cox, Judy. 2004. *Go to Sleep, Groundhog!* New York: Holiday House.

Gibbons, Gail. 2007. *Groundhog Day!* New York: Holiday House.

Name _____ Date _____

Groundhog Day Riddles

Directions: Use the Word Bank to solve the groundhog riddles below.

Word Bank

winter   Phil   spring   veggies

1.  A groundhog likes to eat these.

What are they?

___ ___ ___ ___ ___ ___ ___

- -

___ ___ ___ ___ ___ ___ ___

2. A groundhog sees his shadow.

We will see six more weeks of this.

___ ___ ___ ___ ___ ___

- - - - - - - - - - - - - - - - - - - -

___ ___ ___ ___ ___ ___

3.  A groundhog does not see his shadow.

This will come early.

___ ___ ___ ___ ___ ___

- - - - - - - - - - - - - - - - - - - -

___ ___ ___ ___ ___ ___

Name _____   Date _____

How's the Weather?

Directions: Use the Word Bank to unscramble the weather words below.

Word Bank

cloudy   hot   rainy   windy

1. loucyd

   ___ ___ ___ ___ ___ ___
   -
   ___ ___ ___ ___ ___ ___

2. toh

   ___ ___ ___
   - - - - - - - - - - -
   ___ ___ ___

3. nyrai

   ___ ___ ___ ___ ___
   - - - - - - - - - - - - - - - - - -
   ___ ___ ___ ___ ___

4. ydwin

   ___ ___ ___ ___ ___
   - - - - - - - - - - - - - - - - - -
   ___ ___ ___ ___ ___

Name _____ Date _____

Connect the Groundhogs

Directions: Match each subtraction problem on the left to its answer on the right.

12 − 4 =

10 − 3 =

5 − 2 =

9 − 5 =

11 − 2 =

7

3

8

9

4

#51046—*The Big Book of Holidays and Cultural Celebrations* **37**

Name _____ Date _____

Connect the Weather Words

Directions: Draw a line to match the weather word parts. Use the pictures to help you.

snow

drop

rain

shine

sun

flake

spring

time

um

brella

#51046—*The Big Book of Holidays and Cultural Celebrations*   © *Shell Education*

Name _____ Date _____

Winter or Spring? Pictures

Directions: Look at the images below. Cut and paste each image in the correct column on the *Winter or Spring? Chart* (page 40).

Name _____ **Date** _____

Winter or Spring? Chart

Directions: Paste the _Winter or Spring? Pictures_
(page 39) in the correct column.

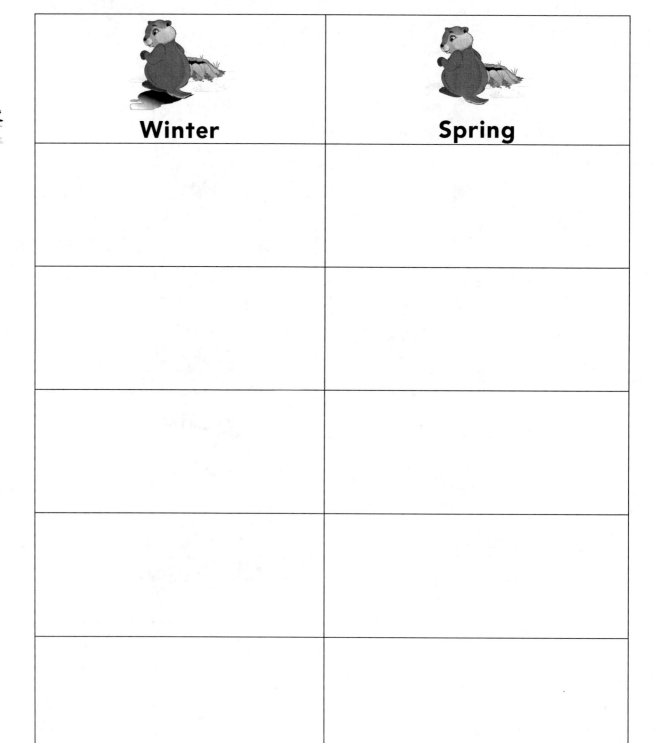

Winter	Spring

Name _____   Date _____

Happy Groundhog Day!

Directions: Give each student one line to read. Have everyone read the last line together.

Reader 1: This groundhog sleeps all winter.

Reader 2: Phil snuggles in his den.

Reader 3: Then February second comes.

Reader 4: The big day's here again.

Reader 5: He pokes his head up slowly

Reader 6: No shadow can be seen.

Reader 7: Spring will soon be here.

Reader 8: The grass will soon be green.

Reader 9: Thank you, Phil.

Reader 10: We want to say,

Reader 11: Have a Happy

Everyone: Groundhog's Day!

Pop-Up Groundhog

Directions: Make the pop-up groundhog.

Materials

- Groundhog Template (page 43)
- crayons or markers
- scissors
- glue
- craft sticks
- paper cups
- light source (e.g., lamp, sun)

Steps

1. Color the Groundhog Template brown. Cut it out.
2. Glue the groundhog to a craft stick.
3. Decorate or color the cup.
4. Make a slit in the bottom of the cup for the stick to slide through.
5. Insert the stick in the bottom of the cup.
6. Place a strong light by the cup.
7. Pop up the groundhog.
8. Use light to create shadows with the groundhog.

Groundhog Template

Lincoln's Birthday
February 12th

Background Information

Abraham Lincoln was born in 1809 in a log cabin in Hardin County, Kentucky. His family moved to Indiana in 1817, squatting on public land until Thomas Lincoln could afford to purchase the land. Nancy Hanks Lincoln died when Lincoln was nine years old. Thomas remarried, and Abraham was fond of his stepmother, Sarah Bush Johnston Lincoln. He had little formal education, probably less than two years. However, he was known for walking miles to borrow a book. Just before receiving the party's nomination for president, he said, "I could read, write, and cipher…but that was all."

When Abraham was old enough, his jobs included splitting wood and working in turn as a rail-splitter, a shopkeeper, a postmaster, and a general-store owner. After serving in the Black Hawk War in 1832, he began his law career. He practiced law in Springfield, Illinois. During his years practicing law, he began to form definite views on slavery and government. He fell in love with Anne Rutledge, who died of typhoid fever. As the years passed, Lincoln became more involved in politics. Distressed by the 1857 Supreme Court ruling that African Americans were not citizens and had no inherent rights, Lincoln decided to run for Senate. His stirring debates against incumbent Senator Stephen Douglas gave him wide exposure. Although he lost that election, he was ready when asked to run for the presidency. Although he received less than 40 percent of the popular vote, he carried the electoral votes. During his first term, Lincoln demonstrated great leadership skills and wisdom. He built a strong cabinet of political rivals. When several states seceded from the Union, he showed greater strength. In spite of opposition from many sides, he commandeered resources and people to preserve the Union and abolish slavery.

Despite the challenges of the war, Lincoln was reelected to a second term. On April 14, 1865, Lincoln visited Ford's Theatre in Washington, D.C. John Wilkes Booth, an actor devoted to the cause of the South, shot Lincoln, who later died. The first formal observance of Lincoln's birthday was held in the Capitol Building in Washington, D.C., on February 12, 1866.

Recommended Books

Kalman, Maira. 2012. *Looking at Lincoln*. New York: Putnam, Nancy Paulsen Books.

Polacco, Patricia. 2011. *Just in Time, Abraham Lincoln*. New York: Putnam.

Winnick, Karen. 1999. *Mr. Lincoln's Whiskers*. Honesdale, PA: Boyds Mill Press.

Name _____   **Date** _____

Abraham Lincoln Riddles

Directions: Use the Word Bank to solve the Abraham Lincoln riddles below.

Word Bank

beard   reading   hat   cabin

1.      This is where Abraham Lincoln was born.

What is it?

___ ___ ___ ___ ___

- - - - - - - - - - - - - - - - - - - -

___ ___ ___ ___ ___

2.      This is how Lincoln learned.

What is it?

___ ___ ___ ___ ___ ___ ___

- - - - - - - - - - - - - - - - - - - -

___ ___ ___ ___ ___ ___ ___

3.   He wore one of these.

What is it?

___ ___ ___

- - - - - - - - - - - - -

___ ___ ___

Connect the Hats

Directions: Match each subtraction problem on the left to its answer on the right.

$10 - 2 =$

4

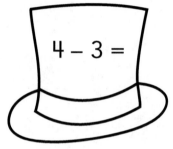

$4 - 3 =$

8

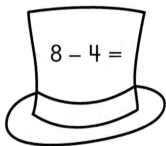

$8 - 4 =$

1

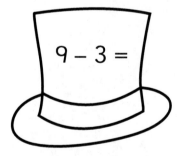

$9 - 3 =$

0

$5 - 5 =$

6

Look Again Lincoln!

Directions: These pictures of a five-dollar bill look a lot alike. Circle the 5 differences on the bill on the right.

Name _____ Date _____

Lincoln Word Search

Directions: Find and circle the words in the Word Bank hidden in the puzzle.

Word Bank

father	log splitter	president
lawyer	postmaster	soldier

a	b	e	p	f	a	t	h	e	r	s
s	r	o	r	p	o	t	n	e	r	c
o	d	c	e	r	l	m	n	u	i	j
l	o	g	s	p	l	i	t	t	e	r
d	f	g	i	j	k	h	v	d	y	u
i	s	g	d	l	a	w	y	e	r	b
e	x	c	e	f	j	i	o	m	l	p
r	u	b	n	e	s	k	n	o	v	d
p	o	s	t	m	a	s	t	e	r	e

#51046—*The Big Book of Holidays and Cultural Celebrations*   © *Shell Education*

Name _____   Date _____

Follow the Penny!

Directions: Start at the penny. Draw a line to connect all of the pennies. Can you get to the five-dollar bill?

Start

Name _____   **Date** _____

Honest Abe

Directions: Give each student one line to read. Have everyone read the last line together.

Reader 1: At first Abe was a lawyer.

Reader 2: But then he chose to run.

Reader 3: To be the country's president.

Reader 4: He was happy when he won.

Reader 5: But then the country went to war.

Reader 6: Some states split away.

Reader 7: Abe got rid of slavery.

Reader 8: And fought to make the states stay.

Reader 9: Abe did a lot of things.

Reader 10: He made sure the war was won.

Reader 11: But someone did not like him.

Reader 12: Too soon, Abe's life was done.

Reader 13: Thank you, Abe.

Reader 14: We want to say,

Reader 15: Have a Happy

Everyone: Abe Lincoln Day!

Design a Stamp

Directions: Make your own stamp for Abraham Lincoln.

Materials

- ruler
- scissors
- construction paper (white and various colors)
- markers or crayons
- glue

Steps

1. Use a ruler to cut a 2" x 3" stamp from white construction paper.

2. Draw a picture to represent Abraham Lincoln, such as showing him reading or working in a store.

3. Choose the cost of the stamp. Write it on the stamp.

4. Glue the stamp onto a colored sheet of construction paper to make a border.

5. Cut the colored construction paper around the stamp to create the border.

Valentine's Day
February 14th

Background Information

Although the exact origins of Valentine's Day are unknown, this holiday has ancient roots. A favorite story is that Emperor Claudius II Gothicus (268–270), also known as Emperor Claudius the Cruel, canceled all engagements and marriages because he wanted young men to become soldiers. A priest by the name of Valentine defied the emperor, performing weddings in secret. Valentine was imprisoned, tortured, and eventually executed on February 14. One variation of this legend says that couples that he married brought him gifts and flowers, a practice that has endured.

By the Middle Ages, Valentine's Day became more associated with romance rather than with martyrdom. Europeans bestowed gifts of confections, flowers, or handmade cards on their lovers. In the 1800s, Esther Howland, who lived in Worcester, Massachusetts, received a valentine from a friend in England. She suggested that her father sell more elaborate cards in his book and stationery store. Esther was inspired to make her own cards, and her father and brother urged her to make cards they could sell. She was one of only a few women in the 1800s to run a successful business.

Today, Valentine's Day is a big business. Nearly one billion cards are exchanged each year. Nearly 200 million red roses, the symbol of love, are purchased. Chocolates are a favorite gift as well. The most famous symbol for the day is Cupid, the son of Venus and the Roman god of love. If Cupid shoots you with an arrow, you are bound to fall in love.

Around the World

Valentine's Day is popular in many countries. In Mexico and other Latin American countries, it is known as the day of love and friendship. Guatemalans celebrate "Affection Day." Chocolates or other gifts are exchanged in South Korea and China. In Japan, women prepare homemade or purchase expensive chocolates for love interests and give more modest chocolates to friends. Men who receive the special chocolates reciprocate with even more elaborate gifts. Residents of South Africa go out to dinner, have dances and balls, and take romantic trips.

Recommended Books

Bond, Felicia. 2006. *The Day It Rained Hearts*. New York: HarperCollins.

Gibbons, Gail. 2006. *Valentine's Day Is…*. New York: Holiday House.

Valentine's Day Riddles

Directions: Use the Word Bank to solve the Valentine's Day riddles below.

Word Bank

cupid   heart   roses   cards

1.   He may make you fall in love.

    Who is he?

    ____ ____ ____ ____ ____

    - - - - - - - - - - - - - - - - - - -

    ____ ____ ____ ____ ____

2.    You may send these.

    What are they?

    ____ ____ ____ ____ ____

    - - - - - - - - - - - - - - - - - - -

    ____ ____ ____ ____ ____

3.    Red ones say "I love you."

    What are they?

    ____ ____ ____ ____ ____

    - - - - - - - - - - - - - - - - - - -

    ____ ____ ____ ____ ____

Roses for You

Directions: Use the Word Bank to unscramble the color of each rose below. Then color the rose that color.

Word Bank

orange   purple   pink   red

1.

plepur

___ ___ ___ ___ ___ ___

2.

ipnk

___ ___ ___ ___

3.

der

___ ___ ___

4.

egnaro

___ ___ ___ ___ ___ ___

Valentine's Day

Connect the Valentine Words

Directions: Draw a line to match the valentine word parts. Use the pictures to help you.

love

ary

cu

birds

Febru

row

ar

pid

flo

wers

Name _____   Date _____

Find Cupid's Heart

Directions: Cupid has lost his heart. Help him find it.
Start at cupid. End at the heart.

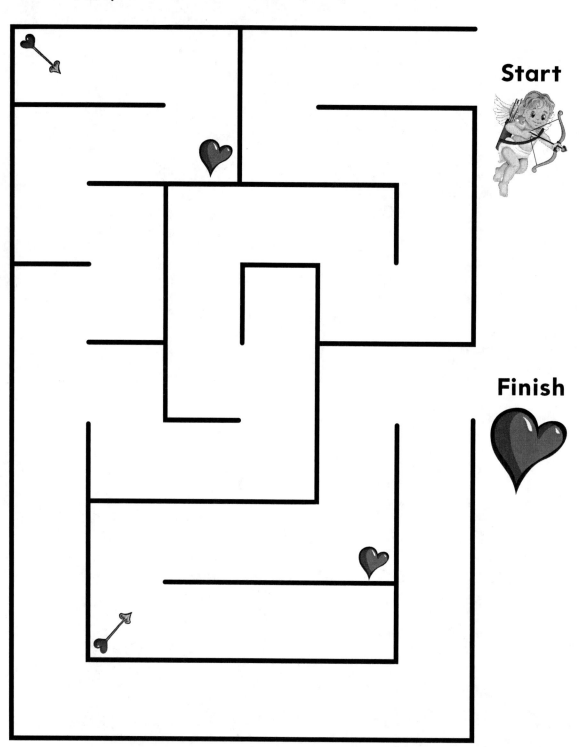

Start

Finish

#51046—*The Big Book of Holidays and Cultural Celebrations*   © *Shell Education*

Connect the Hearts

Directions: Match each addition problem on the left to its answer on the right.

6 + 6 =

9

9 + 5 =

12

3 + 6 =

14

1 + 3 =

11

4 + 7 =

4

Name _____ Date _____

Happy Valentine's Day!

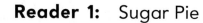

Directions: Give each student one line to read. Have everyone read the last line together.

Reader 1: Sugar Pie

Reader 3: Honey Bun

Reader 4: Cutie Pie

Reader 5: Yum Yum

Reader 6: Write to Me

Reader 7: Here's the key

Reader 8: My Sunshine

Reader 9: On Cloud Nine

Reader 10: Heart of Gold

Reader 110: Heart so Bold

Reader 12: Before we stop,

Reader 13: Let us say...

Reader 14: Have a Happy

Everyone: Valentine's Day!

Hearts in the Round

Directions: Make a wreath out of hearts.

Materials

- construction paper (red, pink, purple, white)
- scissors
- crayons or markers
- paper plate
- glue

Word Bank

Be Mine	Hugs
BFF	Love
Cool	Sweet
Cute	Yours

Steps

1. Cut 3" x 3" squares from colored construction paper.

2. Fold each square and cut out about 12 hearts.

3. Write valentine words on the hearts. Use the Word Bank to help you.

4. Cut a big hole out of the paper plate

5. Place the hearts around the rim of the plate. Glue them down to make a nice pattern for your wreath.

100th Day of School
Date Varies

Background Information

Many schools recognize making it past the halfway point of the year by celebrating the 100th day. Consider beginning the year with some of these activities to build up and honor the day.

From Day 1 to Day 100

- Keep a journal of one significant happening per day for the class. Review it on the 100th day. (If it is too late to start it for this year, keep it in mind for next year.)

- Choose a group challenge with the class, such as reading or exercising 30 minutes a day for 100 days. Other ideas include doing a good deed every day, writing in a daily journal, and picking up trash.

For Day 100

- Consult the website **http://www. history.com/this-day-in-history** to find out what happened 100 years ago on this day in history. Use the information to share events of interest.

- Discuss how much life can change in 100 years. Brainstorm what life might be like 100 years from now.

- Consult **http://thecostofliving.com** to discover average wages plus prices of an apple or a piece of candy 100 years ago. Use the drop down menu at the top to choose the year of comparison. The site also includes inventions and significant events.

- Consult **http://www.foodtimeline. org/WWIprices.pdf** for an overview of food prices for the years 1913 to 1919. This site has more information on historic food prices: **http://www. foodtimeline.org/foodfaq5.html**.

- Collectively generate a list of 100 various things.

Recommended Books

Adler, David A. 2010. *Young Cam Jansen and the 100th Day of School Mystery.* New York: Puffin.

Cuyler, Margery. 2005. *100th Day Worries.* New York: Simon and Schuster.

Murphy, Stuart J. 2003. *100 Days of Cool.* New York: HarperCollins.

Name _____ Date _____

100 Seconds

Directions: What can you do in 100 seconds? Use a clock or a stopwatch. Work with a partner. Do the activity while your partner times you. Then switch roles. Write down how many you did.

Activity	How Many?
Count how many times you can jump rope.	
Count how many sit-ups you can do.	
Count how many times you can say the full alphabet.	
See how high you can count by ones.	
See how high you can count by tens.	
Name as many boys' names as you can.	
Name as many girls' names as you can.	
Name as many animals as you can.	

Name _____   Date _____

My Time Capsule

Directions: Fill the time capsule with drawings of items you would want someone to see 100 years from today.

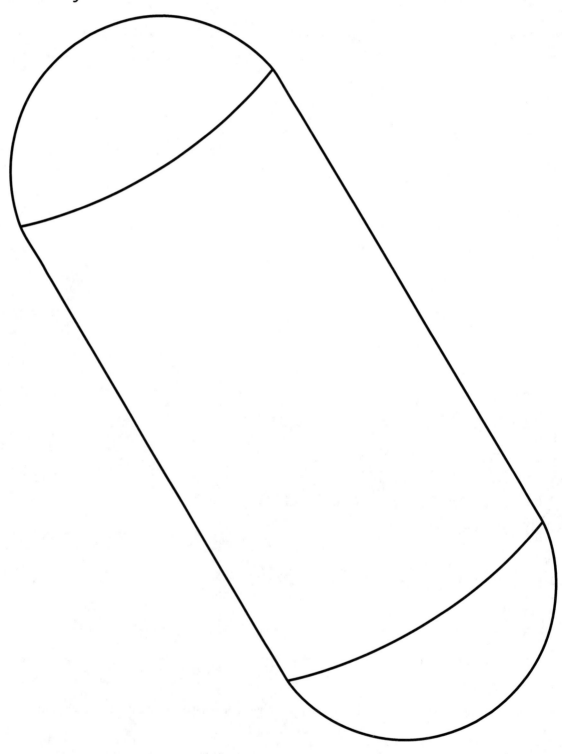

#51046—*The Big Book of Holidays and Cultural Celebrations*   © *Shell Education*

Name _____ Date _____

Make It Better

Directions: There are hundreds of ways we can improve our Earth. Think of the top five. Draw your top five on the Earth below.

#51046—The Big Book of Holidays and Cultural Celebrations **63**

Name _____ **Date** _____

Finish the Poems

Directions: Read the poems. Finish each one. Then create your own.

If I had 100 pennies, this is what I'd do.

_____

- -

I'd get some _____
         for me and for you.

If I had 100 wishes, this is what I'd do.

_____

- -

I'd wish for _____
         for me and for you.

_____

- -

If I had 100 _____
         this is what I'd do.

_____

- -

I'd _____ for me
         and for you.

Name _____ Date _____

Walk to 100

Directions: Work with a partner. Start in the middle of the playground. Do each task below. Have your partner measure how far you went. You will need a long tape measure and a pencil.

What to Do	How Far?
Walk 100 steps.	
Walk 100 giant steps.	
Walk 100 baby steps.	
Hop 100 times.	
Skip 100 times.	
Gallop 100 giant steps.	
Walk backward 100 steps.	
Sidestep 100 times.	

#51046—The Big Book of Holidays and Cultural Celebrations

Name _____ **Date** _____

100 Words

Directions: Read the words below. Work with a group to create a list of 10 words you like about each of the topics. Write your words on a separate sheet of paper. Be sure to number them 1 to 100.

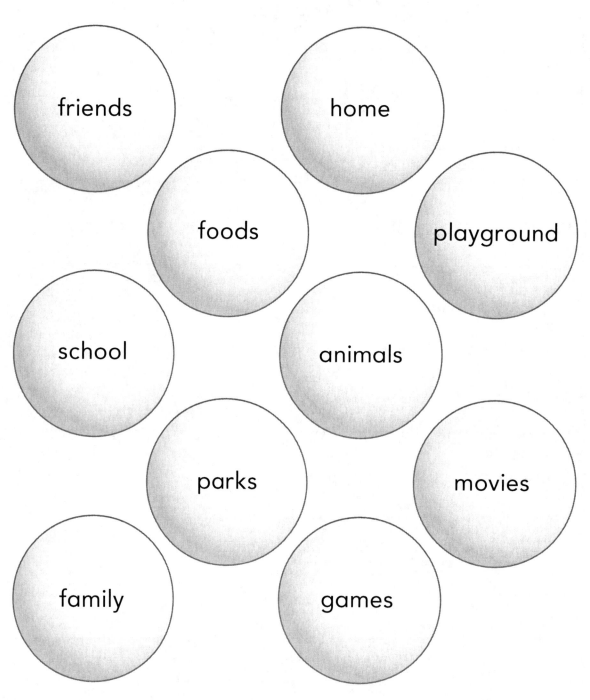

#51046—The Big Book of Holidays and Cultural Celebrations © Shell Education

100 Day Necklaces

Directions: Create a necklace with 100 pieces on it.

Materials

- string
- blue masking tape
- cereal with holes (colored cereal preferred)
- **Note:** Be aware of students' allergies prior to implementation.

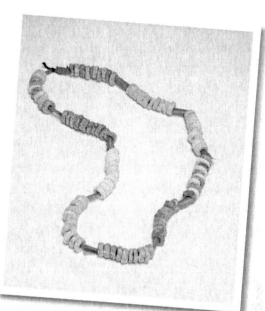

Steps

1. Cut string long enough to create a necklace.

2. Tape one end of the string to the farthest point of your desk.

3. Place 10 pieces of cereal on the string. You may wish to use only one color or create a pattern.

4. Wrap blue masking tape around the string until it is thick enough to make the 10 pieces of cereal stay in place.

5. Continue this process until there are 100 total pieces of cereal on the string.

Presidents' Day
Third Monday of February

Background Information

This holiday originated with our first president, George Washington. The practice of honoring Washington's birth actually began before his presidency. The first celebration, prompted by his military leadership, was held on February 11, 1782, at his Valley Forge headquarters. Because he was born before the adoption of the Gregorian calendar, it wasn't until 1796 that the date of February 22 became accepted as his birthday. The observances grew over the years, with the first public celebration occurring in New York in 1784. During his years of presidency, 1789–1796, the observance became formalized.

Congress passed a resolution after Washington's death on December 14, 1799, that February 22 would be a day of mourning. John Adams continued this observance during his presidency. In 1832, the centenary of Washington's birthday prompted more attention to the date, and 1932 saw even more honors in terms of streets and public buildings named after him. Thirty-two states have

Washington counties. And of course, there is the Washington Monument in Washington, D.C., to commemorate his name.

In 1880, Congress made the day a federal holiday, the first to honor an individual. In 1968, Congress introduced the notion of the Uniform Monday Holiday Bill, which meant that observances such as Washington's Birthday would extend a weekend through Monday. During the debate of the bill, Congress discussed expanding the bill to include Abraham Lincoln's birthday on February 12, which was not celebrated in every state. The final bill was limited to Washington's Birthday. Over time, the day became known as Presidents' Day, and people have come to think of the day as a joint celebration. However, in a few states, Lincoln's birthday is also celebrated.

Recommended Books

Edwards, Roberta. 2009. *Who Was George Washington?* New York: Grosset & Dunlap.

Fritz, Jean. 1998. *George Washington's Breakfast.* New York: Puffin.

Gross, Ruth Belov. 1993. *If You Grew Up with George Washington.* New York: Scholastic.

Keating, Frank. 2012. *George: George Washington, Our Founding Father.* New York: Simon and Schuster/Paula Wiseman Books.

Name _____ **Date** _____

George Washington Riddles

Directions: Use the Word Bank to solve the George Washington riddles below.

Word Bank

tree   February   flag   George

1.  He was our first president.

   What was his first name?

   ___ ___ ___ ___ ___ ___

   ___ ___ ___ ___ ___ ___

2.  Some people think he chopped something down. But that was just a story.

   What was it?

   ___ ___ ___

   ___ ___ ___

3.  He was born in this month.

   What is it?

   ___ ___ ___ ___ ___ ___ ___ ___

   ___ ___ ___ ___ ___ ___ ___ ___

Name _____ Date _____

Presidents Word Scramble

Directions: Use the Word Bank and clues to unscramble the presidential words below.

> **Word Bank**
>
> First Lady   Flag
> Washington   White House

1. stFir   dayL

___ ___ ___ ___ ___   ___ ___ ___ ___

- - - - - - - - - - -   - - - - - - - - -

___ ___ ___ ___ ___   ___ ___ ___ ___

Clue: The title of the President's wife

2. iteWh ouHes

___ ___ ___ ___ ___   ___ ___ ___ ___ ___

- - - - - - - - - - -   - - - - - - - - - - -

___ ___ ___ ___ ___   ___ ___ ___ ___ ___

Clue: Where the President lives

3. toningWash

___ ___ ___ ___ ___ ___ ___ ___ ___ ___

- - - - - - - - - - - - - - - - - - - -

___ ___ ___ ___ ___ ___ ___ ___ ___ ___

Clue: The last name of our first president

4. glaf

___ ___ ___ ___

- - - - - - - -

___ ___ ___ ___

Clue: What we may fly on Presidents' Day

Name _____   **Date** _____

Connect the President Words

Directions: Draw a line to match the President word parts. Use the pictures to help you.

Capi

calen

fl

White Hou

str

tol

ag

dar

se

ipes

The Truth or a Fib?

Directions: The writer who wrote about George Washington cutting down a cherry tree was fibbing. Write two fibs about yourself. Write two truths about yourself. Tell them to a friend. Have him or her guess the truths from the lies.

Fibs About Me

Truths About Me

Name _____   Date _____

Follow the Cherries!

Directions: Start at the cherry. Draw a line to connect all of the cherries. Can you get to the cherry tree?

Start

Name _____ Date _____

Happy Birthday, George!

Directions: Give each student one line to read. Have everyone read the last line together.

Reader 1: George was born in Virginia.

Reader 2: It was 1732.

Reader 3: England ran the colonies.

Reader 4: Who knew George would, too?.

Reader 5: The colonies went to war.

Reader 6: It was 1776.

Reader 7: The country needed a leader.

Reader 8: They knew just whom to pick.

Reader 9: George soon became the president.

Reader 10: He had one more job to do.

Reader 11: He was the father of our country.

Reader 12: That was great for me and you.

Reader 13: Thank you, George.

Reader 14: We want to say,

Reader 15: Have a Happy

Everyone: President's Day!

Design a Flag

Directions: Make a flag to represent the 13 colonies.

Materials

- *Flag Template* (page 76)

- crayons or markers

- scissors

- construction paper (red, white, and blue)

- glue

- 13 star stickers (red, white, or blue)

Steps

1. Choose your colors for the stripes. Color the stripes.

2. Choose the background color for behind the stars. Cut it out and glue it down on the template.

3. Arrange 13 star stickers into a design.

4. Place the flag on the white construction paper.

5. Leave space at the top. Glue it in place.

6. Give your flag a title. Add your name.

Flag Template

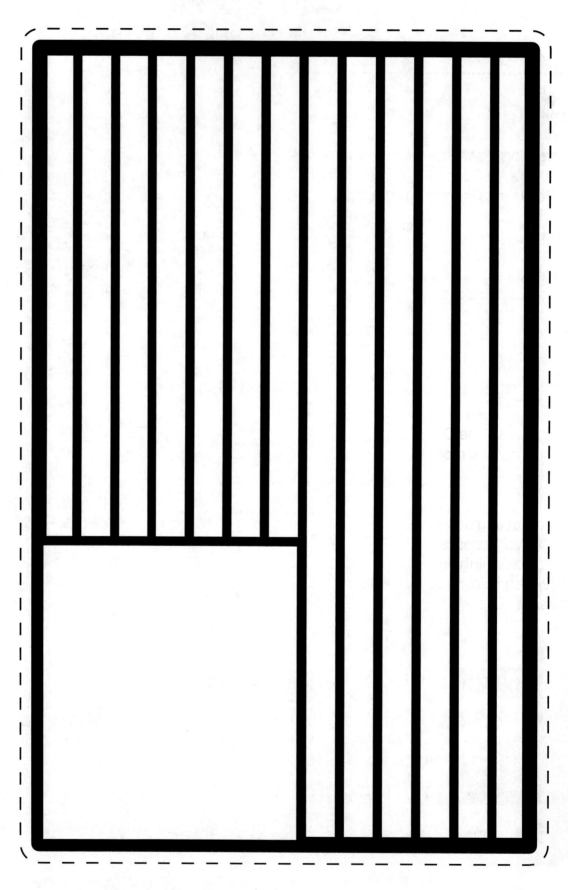

Saint Patrick's Day
March 17th

Background Information

The exact birth date of the patron saint of Ireland is unknown, but it was likely around the year 400 A.D. In his confession, Patrick, whose given name was Maewyn Succat, gives his birthplace as Bannavem Taberniae—without specifying exactly where that is. What is known is that he was captured in Britain by the Gaels and taken by boat to Ireland at the age of 16. He was sold as a slave and tended flocks for six years. He dreamed that he should travel in search of a ship to take him to freedom. A journey of 200 miles led him to the ship, and he landed in Britain, returning home. During another dream, he was urged to return to Ireland to lead the Irish people, then ruled by the Druids, to Christianity. He studied at a monastery in France before returning to Ireland to preach, having taken the name of Patrick by then.

The exact origin of the celebration in the United States is almost as vague as Patrick's birthplace. On March 17, 1762, Irish soldiers serving in the English military marched through New York City.

In 1780, the Friendly Sons of Saint Patrick in Philadelphia celebrated the day, and the New York branch observed the day in 1784. In 1848, several New York Irish Aid Societies united their parades, and that parade continues to be the largest civilian parade in the United States.

On March 17th, "everybody's a little bit Irish." People traditionally wear a bit of green. Shamrocks decorate many stores. And since 1962, the Chicago River turns green for a few hours! Children enjoy thinking about spotting a leprechaun. This cranky, mischievous small fairy works hard as a shoemaker, hiding his gold in pots at the end of the rainbow or in the forest or under rocks.

Around the World

In Ireland, the day is primarily a religious observance, although parades and other activities have been adopted to encourage tourism. Canada, Great Britain, Argentina, New Zealand, Australia, South Korea, Switzerland, Japan, and Singapore also hold celebrations.

Recommended Books

Gibbons, Gail. 1995. *St. Patrick's Day*. New York: Holiday House.

Rockwell, Anne. 2010. *St. Patrick's Day*. Illustrated by Lizzy Rockwell. New York: Harper Collins.

Wing, Natasha. 2009. *The Night Before St. Patrick's Day*. Illustrated by Amy Wummer. New York: Grosset & Dunlap.

Name _____   Date _____

Saint Patrick's Day Riddles

Directions: Use the Word Bank to solve the Saint Patrick's Day riddles below.

Word Bank

| clover | rainbow | Patrick | gold |

1.   You can buy things with it.

What is it?

____ ____ ____ ____

- - - - - - - - - - - - - - - -

____ ____ ____ ____

2. It has many colors.

What is it?

____ ____ ____ ____ ____ ____ ____

- -

____ ____ ____ ____ ____ ____ ____

3.  It has four parts. It brings good luck.

What is it?

____ ____ ____ ____ ____ ____

- -

____ ____ ____ ____ ____ ____

Connect the Clovers

Directions: Match each addition problem on the left to its answer on the right.

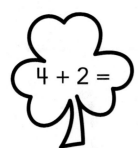 4 + 2 =

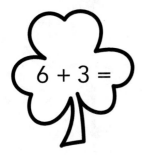 6 + 3 =

 5 + 5 =

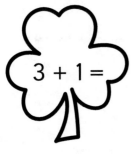 3 + 1 =

 4 + 4 =

 9

 4

 6

 10

 8

Name _____   Date _____

Pot of Gold!

Directions: The leprechaun has hidden the pot of gold. Can you find it? Start at the leprechaun. End at the pot of gold.

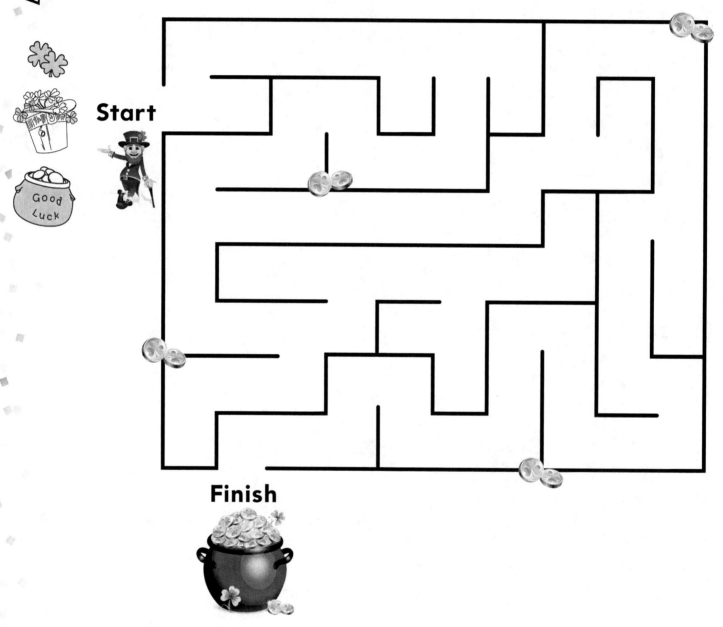

Name _____ **Date** _____

Letters of Gold

Directions: A leprechaun stole all of the vowels from these Saint Patrick's Day words. Write the correct vowels in each word to name the picture.

1.

_____
- - - - -
g _____ ld

2.

_____
- - - - -
p _____ t

3.

_____
- - - - -
sh _____ es

4.

_____
- - - - -
h _____ t

5.

_____   _____
- - - - -   - - - - -
sh _____ mr _____ ck

6.

_____ _____   _____
- - - - - - - - - -   - - - - -
r _____ nb _____ w

Follow the Four-Leaf Clovers!

Directions: Start at the four-leaf clover. Draw a line to connect all of the four-leaf clovers. Can you get to the leprechaun?

Start

Name _____ **Date** _____

A Pot of Gold!

Directions: Give each student one line to read. Have everyone read the last line together.

Reader 1: A leprechaun is very smart.

Reader 2: He saves a lot of gold in a pot.

Reader 3: When a pot got full.

Reader 4: He'd find a hiding spot.

Reader 5: It might be in the forest.

Reader 6: Or at a rainbow's end.

Reader 7: It might be under a rock.

Reader 8: It might be around the bend.

Reader 9: If you can catch a leprechaun.

Reader 10: He has to take you there.

Reader 11: But if you look away,

Reader 12: He'll vanish in thin air.

Reader 13: Now we have to leave you.

Reader 14: Our story has been told.

Reader 15: We're off to find a rainbow

Everyone: And find that pot of gold!

Shamrock Resist

Directions: Create a Saint Patrick's Day shamrock drawing.

Materials

- *Shamrock Template* (page 85)
- green crayon
- green construction paper
- white tempera paint
- water
- paintbrush

Steps

1. Use the *Shamrock Template* to draw shamrocks with green crayon on the green paper. Make the outline heavy.
2. Color lightly inside each shamrock.
3. Mix a small amount of paint with water, Paint a light coating of the mixture on your drawing.
4. Let it dry. Display.

Shamrock Template

Easter
On a Sunday between March 22nd and April 2

Background Information

Easter falls on the Sunday following the first full moon after the vernal equinox. This important observance in the Christian year marks the day that Jesus Christ was resurrected after being hanged on a cross. Christians believe that he saved people through dying. Lent, a period of 40 days (not including Sundays) of fasting and penance ends on Easter. Other key days include Palm Sunday, the Sunday before Easter when Jesus rode triumphantly into Jerusalem; Maundy Thursday, which is associated with the Last Supper and the giving of gifts as symbolized by the washing of feet; Good Friday, the day on which Christ was hanged; and Holy Saturday, when some Christians have baptisms and their first communions.

A variety of customs are observed with some variability in the United States and countries where Christians observe Easter. One of the oldest is the practice of eating hot cross buns on Good Friday. Such buns are considered to be lucky. This may trace back to the time when Egyptians used small loaves in their worship of Isis, the Mother Goddess. The Greeks used cross-marked cakes to honor Diana. The Easter lily is often used to decorate churches or given as a gift. Wearing new clothes, considered particularly lucky if you have three new items, may date from when the New Year was held in March. The new clothes led to the Easter Parade in many communities, with the largest held on Fifth Avenue in New York City.

Perhaps the most popular Easter tradition with children, regardless of religious background, is the Easter bunny. Traditionally, it was a hare, not a rabbit, that was related to Easter. The association developed from the connection of Easter to the phases of the moon and the ancient belief that hares, born with their eyes open, were nocturnal animals that, like the moon, never blinked. Traditions such as decorating eggs and Easter egg hunts provide many fun and exciting memories for families.

Recommended Books

Brett, Jan. 2010. *The Easter Egg.* New York: Penguin.

Kroll, Steven. 2008. *The Biggest Easter Basket Ever.* New York: Cartwheel.

O'Connor, Jane. 2009. *Fancy Nancy's Elegant Easter.* New York: Harper.

Name _____ **Date** _____

Easter Riddles

Directions: Use the Word Bank to solve the Easter riddles below.

Word Bank

basket   cross   eggs   hare

1.   Jelly beans and eggs may come in this.

What is it?

___ ___ ___ ___ ___ ___

- - - - - - - - - - - - - - - - - - - -

___ ___ ___ ___ ___ ___

2.   Children hunt for these on Easter.

What are they?

___ ___ ___ ___

- - - - - - - - - - - - -

___ ___ ___ ___

3.  This was the first Easter animal. It looks like a rabbit.

What is it?

___ ___ ___ ___

- - - - - - - - - - - - -

___ ___ ___ ___

       87

Name _____   **Date** _____

Bunny Word Search

Directions: Find and circle the names of famous rabbits in the Word Bank hidden in the puzzle.

Word Bank

Bugs	FuFu	Velveteen
Bunnicula	Peter	White
	Thumper	

A	E	G	Y	W	P	T	R	I	X
C	F	I	E	H	Y	H	I	S	F
B	U	N	N	I	C	U	L	A	R
U	F	Z	B	T	V	M	X	N	L
G	U	N	C	E	J	P	B	M	V
S	O	W	H	U	Z	E	C	K	U
R	U	P	E	T	E	R	Y	L	A
V	E	L	V	E	T	E	E	N	I

Name _____ Date _____

Connect the Eggs

Directions: Match each subtraction problem on the left to its answer on the right. Then color the eggs.

4 − 2 =   0

5 − 4 =   2

8 − 8 =   4

7 − 3 =   1

9 − 2 =   7

Name _____   Date _____

Fill the Easter Basket

Directions: Color the images that represent Easter and Springtime. Draw an X on the images that do not represent Easter.

#51046—*The Big Book of Holidays and Cultural Celebrations*   © *Shell Education*

Name _____ Date _____

Hop to It!

Directions: Follow the steps to collect the letters. Circle them and write them in the blanks to find the hidden word. The first letter is done for you.

1. Hop 5 spaces to the right.   _____

2. Hop 3 spaces down. - - - - - -

3. Hop 3 spaces to the left. - - - - - -

4. Hop 2 spaces up. _____

5. Hop 7 spaces to the right. - - - - - -

6. Hop 2 spaces down. - - - - - -

Start	a	c	e	i	(b)	p	u	f	u
d	r	k	y	u	s	a	s	a	e
y	l	t	x	o	p	f	b	s	m
t	o	s	t	m	a	p	c	i	t

Easter eggs are kept in a:

_____

- -

_____

  #51046—The Big Book of Holidays and Cultural Celebrations **91**

Easter

Bunny Match-Up

Directions: Play a memory game with the Easter Bunnies.

1. Color two bunnies green, two bunnies pink, and two bunnies yellow.

2. Cut out the cards.

3. Place them facedown. Then take turns flipping them over to find a match.

Easter Placemat

Directions: Make your own Easter placemat or work of art.

Materials

- *Easter Egg* Template (page 94)

- 11" x 17" light construction paper

- scissors

- pencil

- markers or crayons

- contact paper (optional)

Steps

1. Cut out the egg outline.

2. Trace 6 or more eggs on the paper. Have some of them overlap if you wish.

3. Use crayons or markers to color them. Make each one different.

4. Use your art as a placemat. You can also hang it on the wall.

5. You may wish to cover the placemat with contact paper for durability.

Easter Egg Template

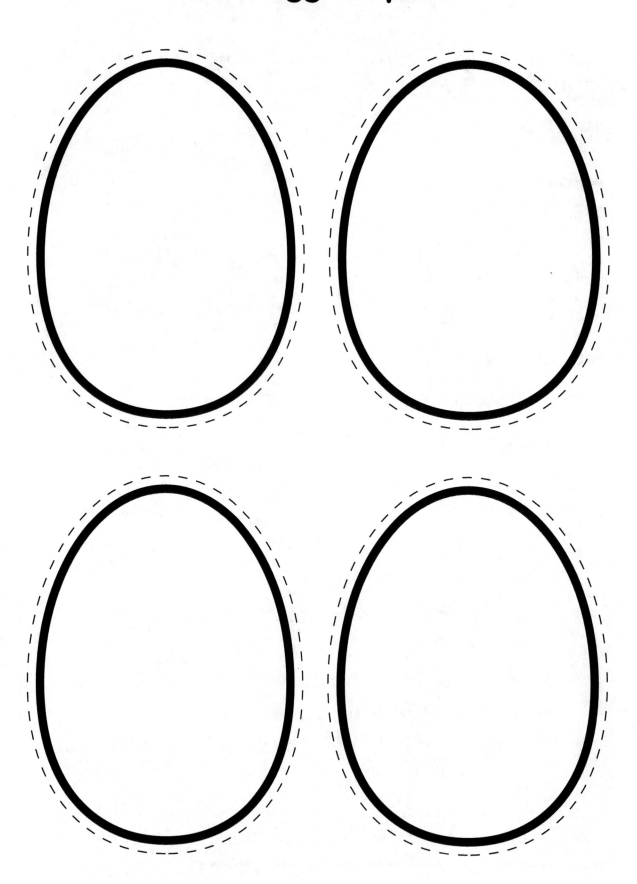

#51046—*The Big Book of Holidays and Cultural Celebrations*

Passover
Seven Days in March or April

Background Information

Passover, *Pesach* in Hebrew, begins on the 10th day of the lunar month of Nisan. The roots of Passover can be found in the 12 chapter of the book of Exodus in the Bible. The Israelites lived peacefully in Ancient Egypt (more than 1,000 years before the Common Era) until a pharaoh made them slaves. Many firstborn children were drowned in the Nile, but Moses was rescued by the pharaoh's daughter. As an adult, Moses realized his heritage and escaped to Sinai (SAHY-nahy). After 40 years, he returned to Egypt to free his people. The pharaoh repeatedly refused a request to let his people celebrate a feast, leading to a series of devastating plagues.

The 10th plague was death by an avenging angel of every firstborn Egyptian son. To prevent their own children's deaths, the Israelites marked their door frames with lamb's blood so the angel would "pass over" their homes. With this, Moses was allowed to lead his people out of Egypt. However, the pharaoh changed his mind, and his army pursued the Israelites to the Red Sea, where the sea parted and they passed through safely. The sea then closed on the soldiers, and Moses led his people to Sinai, called the Promised Land.

While historians and scholars may debate the timing and details of these events, the accounts are the basis for this important Jewish observance. During the seder (SEY-der), a Passover feast, this story is retold while identifying how the special foods relate to the exodus story. Children participate in the telling of the exodus found in the Haggadah (huh-GAH-duh), the story of the flight from Egypt, by asking four significant questions. They also enjoy finding a piece of matzo (MAHT-suh) that is hidden before the seder. One important practice during the Passover observances include eating unleavened bread (matzo), consistent with the bread the Israelites prepared for their flight. Eating bitter herbs commemorates the bitterness of slavery. Wine or grape juice celebrates freedom.

Recommended Books

Aloian, Molly. 2009. *Passover*. New York: Crabtree.

Lehman-Wilzig, Tami. 2006. *Passover Around the World*. Minneapolis, MN: Kar-Ben Publishing.

Levine, Anna. 2012. *Jodie's Passover Adventure*. Minneapolis, MN: Kar-Ben Publishing.

Musleah, Rahel. 2000. *Why on This Night? A Passover Haggadah for Family Celebration*. New York: Puffin.

Name _____ **Date** _____

Seder Time!

Directions: Use the Word Bank to solve the Passover riddles below.

Word Bank

matzo   candles   king   seder

1. People light these for Passover.

   What are they?

   ___ ___ ___ ___ ___ ___ ___

   ___ ___ ___ ___ ___ ___ ___

2. During seder, you eat this.

   What is it?

   ___ ___ ___ ___ ___

   ___ ___ ___ ___ ___

3. This man is a pharaoh. He was a ruler.

   What other person is a ruler?

   ___ ___ ___ ___

   ___ ___ ___ ___

Name _____ Date _____

Passover Foods!

Directions: Use the Word Bank to unscramble the Passover foods below.

Word Bank

celery   matzo   parsley   potato

1. atzom

   ___ ___ ___ ___ ___

   -

   ___ ___ ___ ___ ___

2. slparye

   ___ ___ ___ ___ ___ ___ ___

   -

   ___ ___ ___ ___ ___ ___ ___

3. leceyr

   ___ ___ ___ ___ ___ ___

   -

   ___ ___ ___ ___ ___ ___

4. otapot

   ___ ___ ___ ___ ___ ___

   -

   ___ ___ ___ ___ ___ ___

Name _____   **Date** _____

Connect the Pyramids

Directions: Match each subtraction problem on the left to its answer on the right.

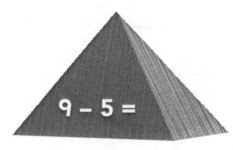 9 − 5 =

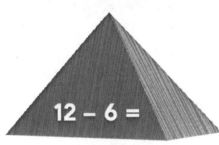 12 − 6 =

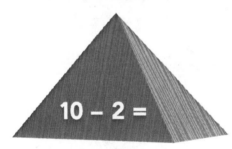 10 − 2 =

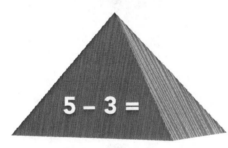 5 − 3 =

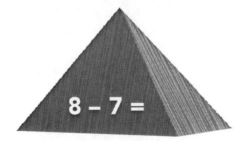 8 − 7 =

 6

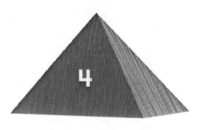 4

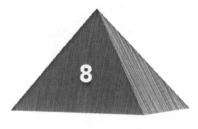 8

 1

 2

#51046—The Big Book of Holidays and Cultural Celebrations   © Shell Education

Crossing the Red Sea

Directions: Help Moses and his people make it to the pyramids.

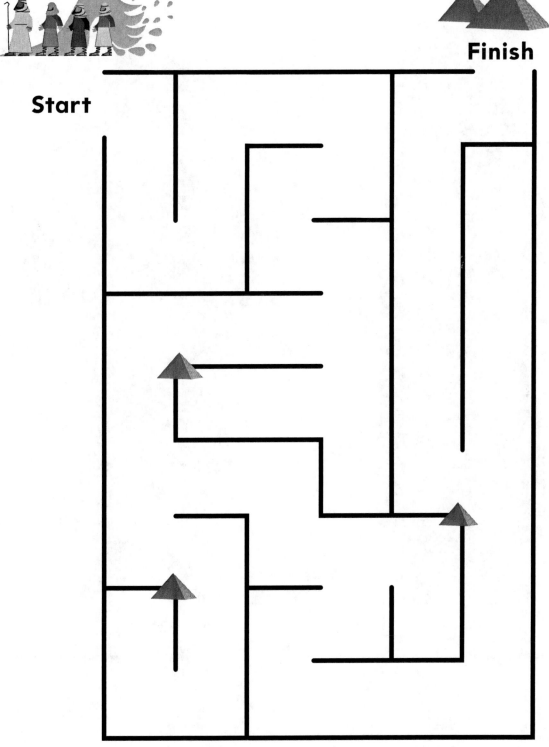

Start

Finish

Name _____ **Date** _____

Look Again Passover!

Directions: These two pharaohs look a lot alike. Circle the 5 differences on the pharaoh on the right.

 #51046—*The Big Book of Holidays and Cultural Celebrations*

Name _____   Date _____

A Passover Story

Directions: Give each student one line to read. Have everyone read the last line together.

Reader 1:   The 10 plagues started coming.

Reader 2:   These were not very nice.

Reader 3:   Frogs were everywhere.

Reader 4:   Everyone got lice.

Reader 5:   Moses asked the pharoah....

Reader 6:   ....to let his people go.

Reader 7:   Everytime Moses asked....

Reader 8:   ...the pharoah answered, "No!"

Reader 9:   The plagues just kept on coming.

Reader 10:   Flies and gnats and hail.

Reader 11:   The last one was the death

Reader 12:   of every firstborn male.

Reader 13:   The Israelites marked their doors

Reader 14:   to let the angel see.

Reader 15:   He passed over their homes

Everyone: And let the firstborns be.

Pyramids of Egypt

Directions: Egypt is known for its huge pyramids. Make a picture of them.

Materials

- paper
- square sheet of sandpaper
- pencil
- crayons

Steps

1. Practice sketching some pyramids on paper with a pencil.
2. When you like your sketch, draw it on the sandpaper with crayons.
3. Color the pyramids in.
4. Color the background to make a desert.

April Fools' Day
April 1st

Background Information

April Fools' Day is not an official holiday. However, it is a favorite day among the young at heart. Historians speculate that the recognized practice of playing pranks dates back to approximately, 1582, in France, when Charles IX adopted the Gregorian calendar. New Year's Day moved from the last week of March to January 1. Because it took weeks for the change to be fully communicated to rural areas—and because some countries resisted adoption for many years—there was confusion regarding the real New Year's Day. (England did not adopt the calendar until 200 years later.) Gifts were historically exchanged during New Year week. Supposedly, pranksters tried to convince people that April 1 was still New Year's Day by giving out mock gifts. Others were reluctant to accept the news about the changes. Those who continued to celebrate on April 1 were called fools.

Another theory is that nature tricked us into thinking spring had arrived with its variable weather. Some speculated that it originated with an ancient New Year festival celebrating the arrival of spring. Others speculated that it began with recognition that Hilaria, the goddess of nature, could indeed be fickle.

Most pranks in the United States are harmless—clocks are set wrong, children are told that there is no school, people are told their shoelaces are untied, etc.

Around the World

In France, the fool is called a *poisson d'avril,* meaning "the April fish." In Scotland, an April fool is called an April *gowk,* which means a cuckoo. The Iranian practice of playing jokes on Norouz, the first Irani calendar month, dates back thousands of years. In England, where playing pranks wasn't established until the 18th century, an April fool is called a *gob,* a *gawby,* or a *gobby.* Indeed, many of the best nationwide pranks have been launched by the British. The most famous is the report about Switzerland's spaghetti harvest, complete with video footage of Swiss farmers harvesting spaghetti, carefully grown to be the right length!

Recommended Books

Bateman, Teresa. 2004. *April Foolishness.* New York: Albert Whitman.

Brown, Marc. 1985. *Arthur's April Fool.* New York: Little Brown.

Hill, Susanna Leonard. 2011. *April Fool, Phyllis.* New York: Holiday House.

Stevenson, James. 1998. *Mud Flat April Fool.* New York: Greenwillow.

April Fools' Riddles

Directions: Can you solve these hink pink riddles? Hink pinks are words with one syllable that rhyme. Hint: Each puzzle uses *pig* or *hog* in the answer.

Example: What do you call a hog on a run? A hog jog.

1.

What is it called when a pig looks for something in the dirt?

___ ___ ___ ___   ___ ___ ___

___ ___ ___ ___   ___ ___ ___

2.

What do you call a huge pig?

___ ___ ___ ___   ___ ___ ___

___ ___ ___   ___ ___ ___ ___

3.

What do you call a piece of wood for a hog?

___ ___ ___   ___ ___ ___

___ ___ ___   ___ ___ ___

Funny Word Connections

Directions: Draw a line to match the funny word parts. Use the pictures to help you.

brain

car

cup

lady

eye

cake

storm

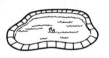

pool

ball

bug

#51046—The Big Book of Holidays and Cultural Celebrations

Name _____ Date _____

Joke Match-Ups

Directions: Cut apart the jokes and the answers. Turn them facedown. Turn two cards over to find a pair.

What kind of hair do oceans have?	wavy
Why does the flamingo only lift up one leg?	If it lifted up two it would fall over.
What is a volcano?	a mountain with hiccups
What runs but never walks?	water
Why did the clock get sick?	It got run down
What is a tornado?	Mother Nature doing the twist
How do you make a milk shake?	Give it a good scare.

April Fools' Search

Directions: Find and circle the funny words in the Word Bank hidden in the puzzle.

Word Bank

funny	giggle	prank	silly
chuckle	laugh	trick	surprise

v	l	g	i	g	g	l	e
w	a	i	z	t	q	x	c
s	u	r	p	r	i	s	e
i	g	w	r	i	p	d	f
l	h	y	a	c	r	s	u
l	r	l	n	k	h	r	n
y	s	m	k	o	j	t	n
c	h	u	c	k	l	e	y

Name _____   Date _____

My Late Day!

Directions: Give each student one line to learn. Have everyone read the last line together.

Reader 1:   I got up late that morning.

Reader 2:   Mom was in a rush.

Reader 3:   She said, "Get dressed for school.

Reader 4:   And don't forget to brush!"

Reader 5:   The toothpaste tasted like salt.

Reader 6:   "April Fool's!" said Dad.

Reader 7:   I ran downstairs for breakfast.

Reader 8:   I thought the joke was fun.

Reader 9:   I was pretty hungry.

Reader 10: But Mom and Dad weren't done.

Reader 11: Mom handed me a plate.

Reader 12: The scrambled eggs were blue.

Reader 13: I poured myself some milk.

Reader 14: They'd made the milk blue, too.

Reader 15: Mom handed me my lunch.

Reader 16: By now, I was scared to look inside.

Reader 17: "Now it's time for school.

Reader 18: Go sit on the front porch.

Reader 19: And wait for the car pool."

Reader 20: I sat there for an hour.

Reader 21: And then I shouted, "Hey!"

Reader 22: My folks had *really* tricked me.

Everyone: It was Saturday!

Happy April to You Poem

Directions: Write an acrostic poem using words that describe April Fools' Day.

A
P
R
I
L
F
O
O
L
S

Trick Card

Directions: Have fun with one of these cards.

Materials

- colored construction paper
- markers or crayons
- glue

Steps

1. Fold the construction paper in half.

2. Choose a message, or think of your own *(Happy April Fools' Day, Happy Spring, Happy April)*

3. Write the message on the front of the card. Decorate with flowers, a rainbow, or something fun.

4. Decorate the back side in the exact same way.

5. Glue the card closed.

6. Give it to someone and watch them try to open it.

7. Shout, "April Fools!" when they are unable to open it.

Earth Day
April 22nd

Background Information

In 1962, Senator Gaylord Nelson from Wisconsin persuaded President John F. Kennedy to conduct a national conservation tour. Although President Kennedy held an 11-state tour on September 1963, the issue of conservation did not take root. Senator Nelson continued to speak on environmental issues for the next several years. During the summer of 1969, in the throes of the general unrest over the Vietnam War, it occurred to Nelson that the time might be right to organize a grassroots demonstration on behalf of the environment. He announced the notion in September 1969, and the response was immediate. The American people were concerned about what was happening to the land, rivers, lakes, and air—and they wanted to voice their concerns. As plans progressed and expanded, John Gardner, founder of Common Cause, joined the effort, with Denis Hayes serving as the coordinator.

On Earth Day 1970, 20 million Americans participated in demonstrations, educational efforts, and cleanups.

Numerous colleges and universities organized rallies and protests. Various groups concerned about a range of issues—polluting factories, oil spills, pesticides, loss of wilderness—came together in a common cause: finding a way to improve Earth. The cause crossed political, social, and economic lines. This effort led to the creation of the Environmental Protection Agency and is credited with prompting the Clean Air Act, Clean Water Act, Endangered Species Act, and other important laws.

In 1990, Earth Day became a global effort. More than 200 million people in 141 countries prompted improved recycling efforts around the world. President Bill Clinton awarded Senator Nelson the Presidential Medal of Freedom in 1995 for his role as the founder of Earth Day.

The Earth Day Network, **http://www. earthday.org**, works with a variety of partners to promote the cause.

Recommended Books

Murphy, Stuart J. 2004. *Earth Day—Hooray!* New York: HarperCollins.

O'Connor, Jane. 2010. *Fancy Nancy: Every Day Is Earth Day.* New York: HarperCollins.

Name _____   **Date** _____

Earth Day Riddles

Directions: Use the Word Bank to solve the Earth Day riddles below.

Word Bank

Earth   litter   recycle   reuse

1.   This is when you take used items and make new things with them.

What is it?

____ ____ ____ ____ ____ ____ ____

- -

____ ____ ____ ____ ____ ____ ____

2.   This word means to use things more than once.

What is it?

____ ____ ____ ____ ____

- -

____ ____ ____ ____ ____

3.   This where we live.

What is it?

____ ____ ____ ____ ____

- -

____ ____ ____ ____ ____

Name _____   **Date** _____

Recycle It!

Directions: Use the Word Bank to unscramble the words below.

Word Bank

cans   glasses   tires   paper

1. erpap

___ ___ ___ ___ ___

- - - - - - - - - - - - - - - - - - -

___ ___ ___ ___ ___

2. irtes

___ ___ ___ ___ ___

- - - - - - - - - - - - - - - - - - -

___ ___ ___ ___ ___

3. snac

___ ___ ___ ___

- - - - - - - - - - - - - - - -

___ ___ ___ ___

4. lagssse

___ ___ ___ ___ ___ ___ ___

- -

___ ___ ___ ___ ___ ___ ___

Earth Day Word Search

Directions: Find and circle the words in the Word Bank hidden in the puzzle.

Word Bank

coffee grounds	peels	leaves	tea bags
eggshells	grass	straw	weeds

b	c	d	e	o	w	p	l	e	a	v	e	s
e	g	g	s	h	e	l	l	s	j	k	l	g
c	o	f	f	e	e	g	r	o	u	n	d	s
r	t	o	t	j	d	l	g	r	u	f	p	t
c	y	u	n	k	s	f	r	e	j	q	j	r
d	n	i	n	o	g	v	a	c	m	s	m	a
v	g	t	p	e	e	l	s	v	n	z	g	w
x	t	e	a	b	a	g	s	x	g	a	n	b

 #51046—The Big Book of Holidays and Cultural Celebrations

Name _____ Date _____

Earth Day—Clean Day

Directions: Color the pictures that show Earth being taken care of. Put an *X* on the pictures that are not taking care of Earth.

Name _____ Date _____

Reduce, Reuse, Recycle!

Directions: Give each student one line to read. Have everyone read the last line together.

Reader 1:   Pick up litter while on your walks.

Reader 2:   Put newspapers in the recycle box.

Reader 3:   Recycle cans and bottles you find.

Reader 4:   Always keep our Earth in mind.

Reader 5:   Plant a tree and watch it grow.

Reader 6:   There's one thing that you should know.

Reader 7:   It cleans more air the bigger it gets.

Reader 8:   That's good for you and for your pets.

Reader 9:   Ride your bike or walk to school.

Reader 10: Helping the Earth is pretty cool.

Reader 11: None of these things are hard to do.

Reader 12: Every day can be Earth Day, too.

Reader 13: It helps everyone to keep our earth clean.

Everyone: Reduce. Reuse. Recycle. Go green!

Connect the Earths

Directions: Match each addition problem on the left to its answer on the right.

 3 + 2 =

 7

 6 + 1 =

 9

 4 + 4 =

 5

 5 + 4 =

 8

 3 + 3 =

 6

Recycle Rainbow

Directions: Use scrap paper and other found objects to make a rainbow.

Materials

- white paper
- scraps of paper in a variety of colors
- glue

Steps

1. Choose four or five colors for the scraps of paper to use for the rainbow.
2. Tear or cut the scraps of paper into small pieces. They can be squares or any shape.
3. Make a small arc with one set of scraps or objects. Glue them in place on the white paper.
4. Make the next arc with a different color.
5. Repeat until the rainbow is finished.
6. Display the rainbow in honor of Earth Day.

May Day
May 1st

Background Information

For some years, children were encouraged to gather a handful of spring flowers and place them in handmade paper baskets. The basket would be left anonymously on a friend's porch. May Day has two distinct holidays: one is for celebration and flowers, the other is meant to be a time to think about workers' rights.

Around the World

Although not an official holiday in the United States, May Day has a long history throughout the world. In ancient times, people celebrated the spring season with festivals. The Romans celebrated from April 28 through May 2 with a feast and a worship of Flora, the goddess of flowers. A tall tree, cut down to be used as the centerpiece of the celebration, became symbolic of May. Sweden celebrated with a mock battle between young men on horseback dressed to represent summer and winter. The Druids of the British Isles marked May 1 with the festival of Beltane, contrasting with Samhain, which fell six months later on November 1. A new year's fire was set, and people walked through the smoke for good luck.

By the Middle Ages, the English had added the Roman's Maypole to the celebration. Villages competed to erect the tallest Maypoles, and dancing accompanied the ritual. Some Maypoles were made permanent, but dancing was periodically forbidden, depending on prevailing royalty and religion of the time. During the May Day festivities, people gathered flowers and branches to decorate their homes, dubbed *bringing in the May*. The May Queen reigned over the festivities. Men danced the morris dance, often in animal-men costumes.

Recommended Books

Cole, Henry. 1997. *Jack's Garden.* New York: Greenwillow.

Ehlert, Lois. 1992. *Planting a Rainbow.* Orlando: Harcourt.

Gibbons, Gail. 1993. *From Seed to Plant.* New York: Holiday House.

Mora, Pat. 2003. *The Rainbow Tulip.* New York: Puffin.

Silverman, Erica. 2011. *On the Morn of Mayfest.* New York: Simon and Schuster.

Name _____   Date _____

May Day Riddles

Directions: Use the Word Bank to solve the May Day riddles below.

Word Bank

basket   flowers   queen   Maypole

1. People like to give these on May Day.

What are they?

_____ _____ _____ _____ _____

- -

_____ _____ _____ _____ _____

2. People would put flowers in this. They would give them as a surprise.

What is it?

_____ _____ _____ _____

- -

_____ _____ _____ _____

3. Sometimes a girl rules over May Day.

What is she called?

_____ _____ _____ _____

- -

_____ _____ _____ _____

Name _____ Date _____

Funny Flower Fun!

Directions: Use the Word Bank to unscramble the funny flower or plant names below.

Word Bank

buttons   dragon tail   butterfly bush

1. fylttbuer   shub

___ ___ ___ ___ ___ ___ ___ ___ ___

- -

___ ___ ___ ___ ___

- - - - - - - - - - - -

___ ___ ___ ___

2. ttbunos

___ ___ ___ ___ ___ ___ ___

- - - - - - - - - - - - - - - -

___ ___ ___

3. radnog   iatl

___ ___ ___ ___ ___ ___

- - - - - - - - - - - - - - - -

___ ___ ___ ___ ___

- - - - - - - - - - - -

___ ___ ___

Find the Maypole

Directions: Help the child find the maypole.

Start

Finish

May Day Jokes

Directions: Cut apart the jokes and the answers. Turn them facedown. Turn two cards over to find a pair.

What flowers are on your face?	tulips
What is a bee's favorite flower?	honeysuckle
What kind of plant did the dishwasher use?	bottlebrush
What is a frog's favorite flower?	crocus
Why couldn't the flower ride a bike?	It had no petals.
How is the letter *A* like a flower?	Both are followed by bees.

Maypole Puzzle

Directions: Anagrams are words that can be rearranged to spell a new word. Use the Word Bank to solve the anagrams of colors below.

Word Bank

rust	lime	ruby	peach
silver	lemon	rose	teal

1. mile _____

2. sore _____

3. sliver _____

4. tale _____

5. ruts _____

6. bury _____

7. melon _____

May Day Math

Directions: Match each addition problem on the left to its answer on the right.

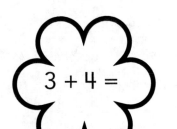 $3 + 4 =$

 4

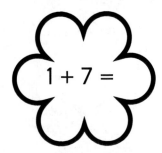 $2 + 2 =$

 7

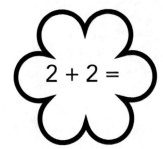 $1 + 7 =$

 9

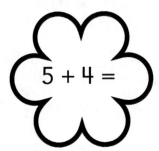 $5 + 4 =$

 8

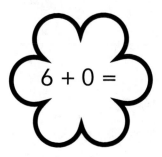 $6 + 0 =$

 6

May Day Basket

Directions: Make a basket and flowers for May Day.

Materials

- *May Day Template* (page 127)
- scissors
- construction paper
- pencil
- tape
- chenille sticks

Steps

1. Cut out and trace the objects from the *May Day Template* onto construction paper.

2. Fold and tape the cone together to make the basket.

3. Tape one end of the construction paper strip on one side of the open end of the cone. Then tape the other end on the other side.

4. Tape each flower to a chenille stick.

5. Put the flowers in the cone.

6. Give your flower basket to someone special.

May Day Template

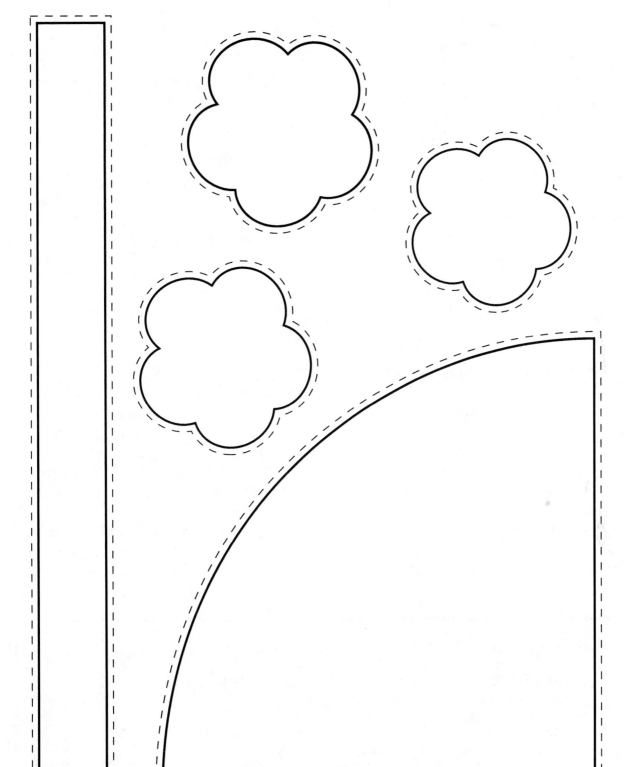

Cinco de Mayo
May 5th

Background Information

After the Mexican-American War of 1846–48, Mexico was facing economic disaster. Their situation worsened during the Mexican Civil War of 1858. They had borrowed heavily, and President Benito Juárez, who became president in 1861, decided Mexico would suspend repayment of debts for at least two years. England, Spain, and France sent naval ships to Veracruz to demand their money. England and Spain withdrew, but Napoleon III saw this as a prime opportunity to add Mexico to his empire.

France sent well-equipped troops to Puebla, Mexico, a small town in east-central Mexico. Expecting a quick victory, France discovered just how powerful the people of Mexico could be. President Juarez patched together a ragtag army half the size of the French troops. However, during the one-day battle, the French lost 500 men and the Mexican forces lost 100. This was a tremendous boost to the spirit of the Mexican people, prompting national unity when the country most needed it.

Unfortunately, Napoleon III was not ready to give up. France did indeed take over Mexico City. Archduke Maximilian of Austria, a relative of Napoleon III, took over the rule of Mexico in 1864. Once the United States' Civil War ended, the United States gave more help to Mexico. The French were ousted, and the Archduke was executed.

Cinco de Mayo recognizes the day of the Battle of Puebla: May 5, 1862. (It should not be confused with Mexican Independence Day of September 16, 1810, when Mexico declared its independence from Spanish rule.) The day is particularly important for Mexican Americans, who pause to enjoy the traditions, music, and food of Mexico. Events such as parades or fiestas are especially festive in communities with large Latino populations. Families may have parties, eat special foods, and make piñatas. Like people who are all "a little bit Irish" on Saint Patrick's Day, people of all backgrounds enjoy the festivities that come with Cinco de Mayo.

Recommended Books

Ada, Alma Flor and F. Isabel Compoy. 2006. *Celebrate Cinco de Mayo with the Mexican Hat Dance*. Miami: Alfaguara Infantil.

Doering, Amanda. 2006. *Cinco de Mayo: Day of Mexican Pride*. Mankato, MN: Capstone.

McKissack, Fredrick L. and Lisa Beringer McKissack. 2000. *Cinco de Mayo—Count and Celebrate!* Berkeley Heights, NJ: Enslow.

Torpie, Kate. 2008. *Cinco de Mayo*. New York: Crabtree.

Name _____   **Date** _____

Cinco de Mayo Riddles

Directions: Use the Word Bank to solve the Cinco de Mayo riddles below.

Word Bank

fiesta   flag   piñata   Mexico

1.  Cinco de Mayo is to remember the battle long ago in what country?

____ ____ ____ ____ ____ ____

- -

____ ____ ____ ____ ____ ____

2.  This is flown in Mexico. Its colors are red, white, and green.

What is it?

____ ____ ____ ____

- - - - - - - - - - - - - - - - -

____ ____ ____ ____

3.  Mexico won the war at last. People have a big party on May 5th to celebrate.

What is the name of the party?

____ ____ ____ ____ ____ ____

- -

____ ____ ____ ____ ____ ____

Spanish and English

Directions: Some Spanish words sound like English words. Write the words from the Word Bank in the correct columns below.

English Word Bank		Spanish Word Bank	
bank	jar	banco	jarra
band	rose	banda	rosa

		English	Spanish
1.		_____	_____
2.		_____	_____
3.		_____	_____
4.		_____	_____

 #51046—The Big Book of Holidays and Cultural Celebrations

Name _____   Date _____

Look Again Cinco de Mayo!

Directions: These pictures look a lot alike. Circle the 5 differences in the group on the bottom.

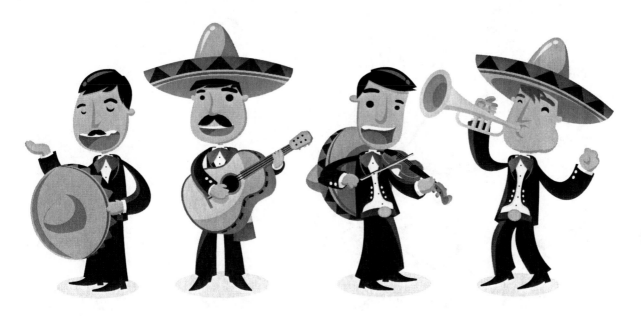

Piñata Time

Directions: It is lots of fun to break a piñata at a fiesta. Fill this piñata with fun things.   Draw five things in the piñata.

Name _____ **Date** _____

Fiesta Food Fun

Directions: Rearrange the letters in each word below to make a new word that matches the picture.

1.

coat _____

_____

_____

2.

miles _____

_____

_____

3.

pagers _____

_____

_____

4.

urbrito _____

_____

_____

5.

cheap _____

_____

_____

Name _____ Date _____

Connect the Maracas

Directions: Match each subtraction problem on the left to its answer on the right.

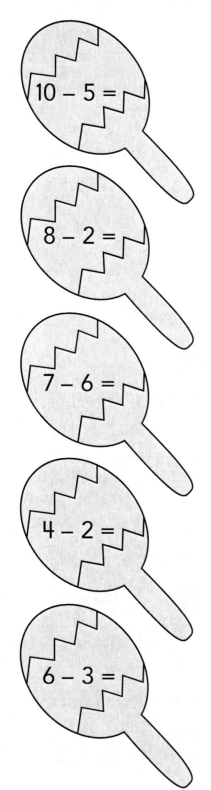

10 – 5 =

8 – 2 =

7 – 6 =

4 – 2 =

6 – 3 =

6

1

5

3

2

Mexican Flag

Directions: Make a colorful flag to celebrate Cinco de Mayo.

Materials

- *Mexican Flag Template* (page 136)

- construction paper

- red, white, and green tissue paper

- glue

- craft stick

- scissors

Steps

1. Cut out the *Mexican Flag Template*.

2. Glue the flag onto construction paper. Then cut out the flag again.

3. Put glue on the left section of the flag. Put torn pieces of green tissue paper on the glue.

4. Repeat this process with the middle section (white paper) and the right section (red paper).

5. Glue a craft stick to the left side of the flag.

Mexican Flag Template

Mother's Day
Second Sunday in May

Background Information

Mother's Day in the United States is approximately 100 years old. However, scholars tie the day to ancient times. The worship of the mother goddess, Cybele began in Rome, approximately 250 B.C.E. The month of March included a series of festivals that concluded with Hilaria, the festival of joy in honor of Cybele. This religious festival differs from our current honoring of mothers.

The early Church honored the Mother of God, Mary, on the fourth Sunday in Lent. Although its time of origin is unknown, young men and women in England who were apprenticed and therefore away from home for long periods of time in the 18th and 19th centuries began returning to their homes on Mothering Sunday. They would bring small tokens of affection, such as cakes or nosegays of violets. Families attended church together and had a dinner, with the mother honored as a queen. This practice was called to *go a-mothering*.

In the United States, Mother's Day can be traced to Anna M. Jarvis (1864–1948). A devoted daughter, Miss Jarvis decided after her mother's death to establish a Mother's Day. She worried that mothers of adult children were neglected and hoped that having a Mother's Day would foster recognition of the sacrifice of mothers. The first Mother's Day observances were church services held in Philadelphia and Grafton, West Virginia, on May 10, 1908. Miss Jarvis supplied carnations at the Grafton service. Over time, red carnations were worn in honor of a living mother, and white carnations were worn for a mother who had died.

By 1911, Mother's Day proclamations had begun to spread across the country. By 1913, President Woodrow Wilson issued the first presidential proclamation, a practice that continues yearly.

Around the World

By 1911, observances were celebrated in Mexico, Canada, China, Japan, and Africa. The Mother's Day International Association was established in late 1912. Although it has spread to more countries, some celebrate it on different days.

Recommended Books

Anderson, Laurie Halse. 2001. *No Time for Mother's Day*. Park Ridge, IL: Albert Whitman.

Balian, Lorna. 2004. *Mother's Mother's Day*. Cambridge, MA: Star Bright.

Bunting, Eve. 1988. *The Mother's Day Mice*. New York: Sandpiper.

Eastman, P.D. 1960. *Are You My Mother?* New York: Random House.

Name _____ **Date** _____

Ways to Say Mom

Directions: Use the ways to say *mom* in the Word Bank to help you unscramble the words below.

Word Bank

ma	mom	mother
mama	mommy	mum

1. omm

_____

- - - - - - - - - - -

_____

2. omrthe

_____

- - - - - - - - - - -

_____

3. mmmoy

_____

- - - - - - - - - - -

_____

4. amam

_____

- - - - - - - - - - -

_____

5. am

_____

- - - - - - - - - - -

_____

6. umm

_____

- - - - - - - - - - -

_____

Name _____ **Date** _____

Animal Moms

Directions: Use the Word Bank to solve the animal-mom riddles below.

Word Bank

alligator   elephant   koala

1. This mom has the biggest baby on land.

   What is it?

   ___ ___ ___ ___ ___ ___ ___ ___

   -

   ___ ___ ___ ___ ___ ___ ___ ___

2.  This mom keeps her baby in her pouch for six months.

   What is it?

   ___ ___ ___ ___ ___ ___

   -

   ___ ___ ___ ___ ___ ___

3.  This mom carries her babies in her jaw.

   What is it?

   ___ ___ ___ ___ ___ ___ ___ ___ ___

   -

   ___ ___ ___ ___ ___ ___ ___ ___ ___

Mother Palindrome Fun

Directions: The word *mom* reads the same way forward and backward. Those words are called *palindromes*. Use the Word Bank to figure out the palindromes below.

Word Bank

bib	mom	eye
tot	pop	Bob

1. It's a word for a mommy.	**2.** It's another word for a father. It's also a word for a soft drink.	**3.** It's what you see with.
_ o _	_ o _	_ y _
4. It's a word for a little kid.	**5.** It's a boy's name.	**6.** It's what a baby wears to keep clean when eating.
_ o _	_ o _	_ i _

A Poem for Mother

Directions: Write an acrostic poem about your mother using words that describe her.

M _____

O _____

T _____

H _____

E _____

R _____

Find the Mother

Directions: Help the child find her mother.

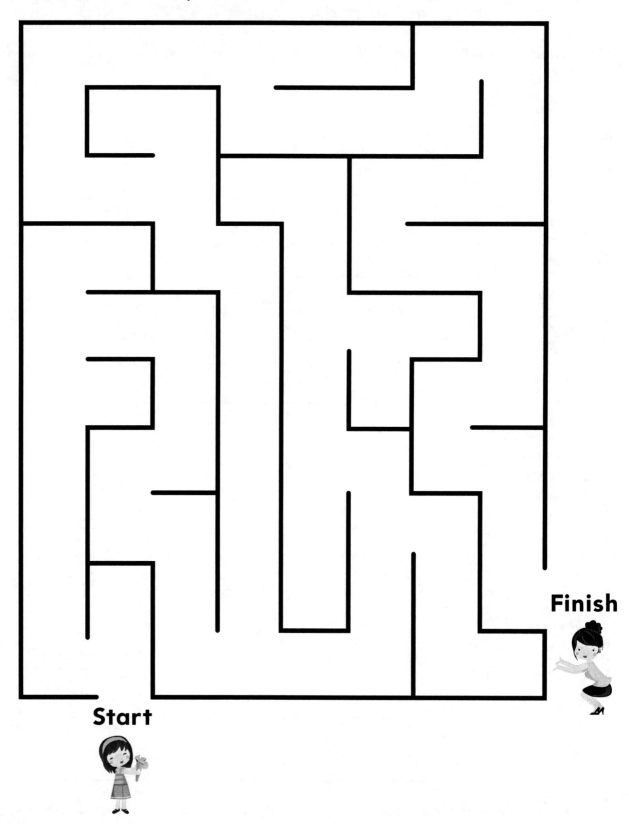

Start

Finish

Name _____ Date _____

All Sorts of Moms

Directions: Give each student one line to read. Have everyone read the last line together.

Reader 1:   Some moms give kisses.

Reader 2:   Some moms give hugs.

Reader 3:   Some moms get rid of

Reader 4:   Big, scary bugs.

Reader 5:   Some moms get the monsters.

Reader 6:   From under your bed.

Reader 7:   Some moms tuck you in

Reader 8:   With a kiss on the head.

Reader 9:   Some moms get tired.

Reader 10: Moms don't get much sleep.

Reader 11: This Mother's Day morning

Reader 12: I won't make a peep!

Reader 13: Here's to all moms.

Reader 14: We want to say,

Reader 15: Have a happy and

Everyone: restful Mother's Day!

Mother's Day Bookmark

Directions: Make a bookmark for Mom.

Materials

- 6" x 2" construction paper
- two or three small flowers and/or leaves, pressed until dry
- markers
- glue
- yarn or ribbon
- contact paper
- hole punch

Steps

1. Arrange the dried flowers on construction paper.
2. Glue in place.
3. Add a stem or leaves with marker, if desired.
4. Cover the bookmark with contact paper.
5. Punch a hole in the top of the bookmark with the hole punch.
6. Loop the ribbon or yarn through the hole. Tie a knot.

Memorial Day
May 30th

Background Information

Memorial Day observances in the United States began shortly after the Civil War, honoring the war dead of both sides. The official birthplace of Memorial Day, previously known as Decoration Day, is Waterloo, New York, where Henry C. Welles recommended decorating soldiers' graves in 1865. A committee worked out the details: flags at half-mast, flowers on graves, black mourning draperies, a parade, and speakers at the cemeteries. Other early observances occurred in Columbus, Mississippi; Boalsburg, Pennsylvania; and Belle Isle in the James River in Richmond, Virginia.

By 1868, ceremonies were held at the National Cemetery in Arlington, Virginia. New York was the first state to legalize the holiday. May 30 may have been chosen as the official date because it is the approximate anniversary of the surrender of the last Confederate Army. The observances of Memorial Day were important for healing the country's rift during the Civil War, which persisted even after the two world wars.

The official name of the holiday is Decoration Day, referring to the decorating of graves. Over the years, the day has come to be one of honoring all ancestors and loved ones who have died in war. Parades and ceremonies may feature members of the military, groups of children from groups such as the Boy Scouts and Girl Scouts of America, and marching bands.

Perhaps the biggest event on Memorial Day is the 500-mile race at the Indianapolis Motor Speedway.

Around the World

Australia and New Zealand honor their soldiers on Anzac Day. The countries of the Commonwealth (formerly British Commonwealth) observe Remembrance Day, also known as Poppy Day or Armistice Day, in honor of those who died in World War I.

Recommended Books

Ansary, Mir Tamim. 2007. *Memorial Day*. Mankato, MN: Heinemann-Raintree.

Dean, Sheri. 2010. *Memorial Day*. New York: Gareth Stevens.

Raven, Margot Theis. 2011. *America's White Table*. Chelsea, MI: Sleeping Bear Press.

Trueit, Trudi Strain. 2007. *Memorial Day*. Mankato, MN: Child's World.

Name _____ **Date** _____

Memorial Day Riddles

Directions: Use the Word Bank to solve the Memorial Day riddles below.

Word Bank

flag   grave   May   picnic

1.   People display this on Memorial Day.

What is it?

___ ___ ___ ___

- - - - - - - - - - - - - - -

___ ___ ___ ___

2.   People put flowers here on Memorial Day

What is it?

___ ___ ___ ___ ___

- - - - - - - - - - - - - - - - -

___ ___ ___ ___ ___

3.   Memorial Day is in this month.

What is it?

___ ___ ___

- - - - - - - - - - -

___ ___ ___

Name _____   Date _____

Memorial Day Words

Directions: Use the words in the Word Bank to unscramble the words below.

Word Bank

| eagle | grave | jeep | medal |

1.

peje   _____ _____ _____ _____

- - - - - - - - - - - - - - - - - -

_____ _____ _____ _____

2.

geale   _____ _____ _____ _____ _____

- - - - - - - - - - - - - - - - - -

_____ _____ _____ _____ _____

3.

damel   _____ _____ _____ _____ _____

- - - - - - - - - - - - - - - - - -

_____ _____ _____ _____ _____

4.

agrev   _____ _____ _____ _____ _____

- - - - - - - - - - - - - - - - - -

_____ _____ _____ _____ _____

Name _____   **Date** _____

Memorial Day Line Up!

Directions: Put the Memorial Day groups below in alphabetical order for the parade.

Word Bank

soldiers	veterans	floats
band	Girl Scouts	drummers

---

1. _____

   _____

2. _____

   _____

3. _____

   _____

4. _____

   _____

5. _____

   _____

6. _____

   _____

Name _____   **Date** _____

Connect the Medals

Directions: Match each addition problem on the left to its answer on the right.

$1 + 4 =$

$4 + 2 =$

$3 + 5 =$

$8 + 1 =$

$5 + 5 =$

6

5

10

8

9

Memorial Day Search

Directions: Find and circle the words in the Word Bank hidden in the puzzle.

Word Bank

flag	grave	war
picnic	veteran	medals
peanuts	jeep	biscuit

f	a	l	t	p	o	r	k	p	m
l	k	w	l	j	c	x	b	i	e
a	a	a	n	e	d	m	i	c	d
g	p	r	u	e	h	j	s	n	a
f	h	a	r	p	t	a	c	i	l
f	n	m	b	v	x	g	u	c	s
v	e	t	e	r	a	n	i	y	f
e	l	p	e	a	n	u	t	s	v
p	o	t	a	t	g	r	a	v	e

Name _____   Date _____

Follow the Eagles!

Directions: Start at the eagle. Draw a line to connect all of the eagles. Can you get to the flag?

Start

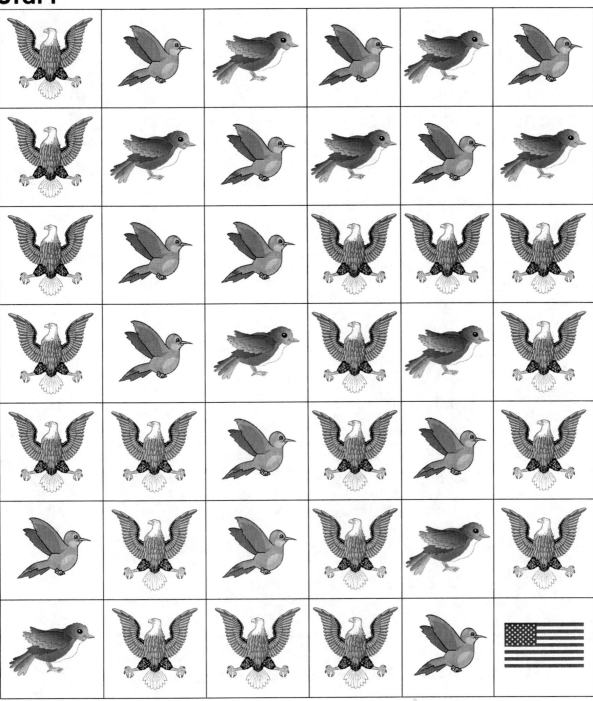

Memorial Day Poppies

Directions: Make poppies to display on Memorial Day.

Materials

- *Memorial Day Template* (page 153)
- red and white construction paper
- black puffballs
- green chenille sticks
- glue
- scissors
- pencil

Steps

1. Copy the hearts from the *Memorial Day Template* onto red construction paper.

2. Cut out 4 hearts.

3. Arrange the poppies (hearts) like the example.

4. Glue the points of the hearts together. Add the black puffball on top.

5. Make several poppies. Arrange each one on white paper to make a design.

6. You can add green chenille sticks for stems.

Memorial Day Template

Father's Day
Third Sunday in June

Background Information

While there are no records of festivals to honor fathers, the ancient Romans did have *Parentalia*, which lasted for more than a week in February. The festival honored departed parents and relatives to "appease the souls of your fathers," according to Ovid, an ancient Roman poet. Families would gather in a sort of reunion. Graves were decorated with offerings such as wine and honey left for the departed on the last day of the festival.

Like Mother's Day, Father's Day originated in the early years of the 20th century in the United States. The first record of a day for fathers is July 5, 1908, when a Father's Day church service was held in West Virginia. Sonora Dodd thought of having a Father's Day while listening to a sermon on Mother's Day in 1909. Her father, William Jackson Smart, had raised six children after the death of his wife. Mrs. Dodd fostered the idea in Spokane, Washington, and the first citywide observation was held on the third Sunday in June in 1910. Mrs. Dodd suggested wearing a white rose for a dead father and a red rose for a living father.

Interest in Father's Day increased as word spread about the Spokane event. However, unlike Mother's Day, it was many years before the day became formalized. In 1924, President Calvin Coolidge recommended that it be "noted" in the states. He would not issue a formal proclamation, even though Mother's Day had been formalized in 1913 by President Woodrow Wilson. Resolutions were introduced into Congress, but it wasn't until 1972 when President Richard Nixon signed a Congressional resolution that the day caught up to Mother's Day.

Fathers are given cards and gifts, with clothes, electronics, tools, and sporting goods being the most popular. Uncles, grandfathers, and men who fill the role of a father are often honored as well.

Around the World

Father's Day is celebrated in many countries around the world, many on the same day as in the United States. In Australia, South Africa, and the United Kingdom, organized groups often gather to celebrate, with children urged to honor their dads.

Recommended Books

Browne, Anthony. 2001. *My Dad*. New York: Farrar, Straus and Giroux.

Bunting, Eve. 1993. *A Perfect Father's Day*. New York: Sandpiper.

Gikow, Louise A. 2004. *A Day with Daddy*. New York: Children's Press.

Name _____   **Date** _____

Ways to Say Dad

Directions: Use the ways to say *dad* in the Word Bank to help you unscramble the words below.

```
                        Word Bank
        dad            daddy          papa
        dada           father         pop
```

1. add

_____

- - - - - - - - - - - - -

_____

2. rafthe

_____

- - - - - - - - - - - - -

_____

3. adddy

_____

- - - - - - - - - - - - -

_____

4. adda

_____

- - - - - - - - - - - - -

_____

5. ppo

_____

- - - - - - - - - - - - -

_____

6. apap

_____

- - - - - - - - - - - - -

_____

Name _____   **Date** _____

Animal Dads

Directions: Use the Word Bank to solve the animal dad riddles below.

Word Bank

frog   lion   penguin

---

1.   This dad likes to nap. But he also watches his cubs.

What is he?

____ ____ ____ ____

- - - - - - - - - - - - - - - - - -

____ ____ ____ ____

2.   This dad swallows the eggs for six weeks. Then he spits them out when the babies are ready to be born!

What is he?

____ ____ ____ ____

- - - - - - - - - - - - - - - - - -

____ ____ ____ ____

3.    This dad keeps the egg warm for months. He does not even eat!

What is he?

____ ____ ____ ____ ____ ____ ____

- -

____ ____ ____ ____ ____ ____ ____

Name ______________________ Date ______________

A Poem for Father

Directions: Write an acrostic poem about your father using words that describe him.

F

A

T

H

E

R

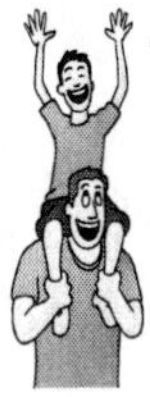

Name _____ Date _____

Father's Day Search

Directions: Find and circle the words for father in the Word Bank hidden in the puzzle.

Word Bank

dad	father	pop
daddy	grandfather	poppa
	papa	

p	o	d	a	n	a	d	a	t	e	s
g	r	a	n	d	f	a	t	h	e	r
m	o	d	p	o	a	d	k	a	l	m
p	o	p	p	a	t	d	d	i	d	n
o	s	t	a	f	h	y	o	y	t	b
p	u	v	p	d	e	e	u	m	v	l
c	i	l	a	d	r	d	a	f	h	e

#51046—The Big Book of Holidays and Cultural Celebrations   © Shell Education

Name _____   Date _____

Connect the Ties

Directions: Match each subtraction problem on the left to its answer on the right.

All Sorts of Dads

Directions: Give each student one line to read. Have everyone read the last line together.

Reader 1: Some dads give hugs.

Reader 2: Or pats on the back.

Reader 3: Some fix your dinner.

Reader 4: Some make your snack.

Reader 5: Some dads read you stories.

Reader 6: When you go to bed.

Reader 7: Some bring you water.

Reader 8: And kiss you on your head.

Reader 9: Some dads get cranky.

Reader 10: Dads don't get much rest.

Reader 11: But that doesn't matter.

Reader 12: My Dad's the best!

Reader 13: Here's to all dads.

Reader 14: We want to say,

Reader 15: Have a Happy and

Everyone: Restful Father's Day!.

Pencil Holder for Dad

Directions: Make a special pencil holder for your dad.

Materials

- paper cup
- wrapping paper or construction paper
- tape
- decorative stickers
- markers or crayons

Steps

1. Lay the paper on a flat surface. Mark it so that it is the height of the cup. Roll the cup along the paper to see how much you will need to go around it.

2. Cut out the paper so that it will wrap around the cup.

3. Decorate the paper. If your dad loves a sport, you may want to use that sport for your theme. Tape the paper to the cup.

4. Put a few pencils in the cup.

5. Give as a gift for Father's Day.

Independence Day
July 4th

Background Information

July 4, 1776, is considered the birthday of the United States. In the 15 previous years, opposition to the English rule had been growing. While there had been riots in opposition to the Stamp Act, it was Parliament's passing of the Townshend Acts in June of 1767 that triggered the most resentment. These import duties on tea, glass, painters' colors, oil, lead, and paper were to pay for the salaries of the royal governors and judges in the colonies.

On March 5, 1770, tempers flared in Boston. British soldiers were stoned by a mob and fired back, killing several citizens. Known as the Boston Massacre, this event prompted the repeal of all the import duties with the exception of tea. Later that year, on December 16, the Boston Tea Party occurred. Disguised as Mohawk American Indians, men boarded English ships and tossed the cargo of tea into the Boston Harbor. The British retaliated with the passage of the Intolerable Acts, which included in part the closure of the Boston port and outlawed unsanctioned public meetings.

On September 5, 1774, the First Continental Congress met in Philadelphia and adopted a Declaration of Rights, including the rights of life, liberty, and property. Battles such as Lexington and Concord began, signaling the beginning of the war. Upon the publication of Thomas Paine's *Common Sense,* the colonies began the push toward independence. Thomas Jefferson was appointed to draw up the Declaration of Independence. The colonies decided on July 2 that they should be free and independent states. Two days later, the Declaration of Independence was endorsed by John Hancock, president of Congress, and Charles Thomson, secretary.

The first Independence Day was celebrated in 1777 in Philadelphia. The observation included ringing bells, fireworks, bonfires, ships firing 13-gun salutes, and lighted candles in home windows. Massachusetts voted official recognition of the holiday in 1781. The Fourth of July was celebrated in the territories as well. It became a national holiday nearly 100 years later, in 1870.

Recommended Books

Heiligman, Deborah. 2007. *Holidays Around the World: Celebrate Independence Day: With Parades, Picnics, and Fireworks.* Washington, DC: National Geographic Children's Books.

Landau, Elaine. 2008. *The Declaration of Independence.* New York: Children's Press.

Landau, Elaine. 2011. *What Is the 4th of July?* Berkeley Heights, NJ: Enslow.

Name _____ **Date** _____

Independence Day Riddles

Directions: Use the Word Bank to solve the Independence Day riddles below.

Word Bank

July 4	flag	tea	uniform

1.  We say this date is our country's birthday.

What is it?

____ ____ ____ ____ ____

____ ____ ____ ____ ____ _ _ _ _ _

____ ____ ____ ____ ____

2. This represents a country.

What is it?

____ ____ ____ ____

____ ____ ____ ____ ____ ____ ____

____ ____ ____ ____

3. The British wanted to tax this a lot.

What is it?

____ ____ ____

____ ____ ____ ____

____ ____ ____ ____

Birthday of a Nation Words

Directions: Use the words in the Word Bank to unscramble the words below.

Word Bank

concert   parade   sparklers

fireworks   picnic

1. cipinc

___ ___ ___ ___ ___ ___

\- -

___ ___ ___ ___ ___ ___

2. riewofksr

___ ___ ___ ___ ___ ___ ___ ___ ___

\- -

___ ___ ___ ___ ___ ___ ___ ___ ___

3. aardep

___ ___ ___ ___ ___ ___

\- -

___ ___ ___ ___ ___ ___

4. pssrrakle

___ ___ ___ ___ ___ ___ ___ ___ ___

\- -

___ ___ ___ ___ ___ ___ ___ ___ ___

5. ccnoret

___ ___ ___ ___ ___ ___ ___

\- -

___ ___ ___ ___ ___ ___ ___

Connect the Flags

Directions: Match each subtraction problem on the left to its answer on the right.

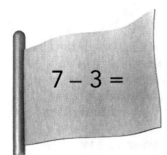
7 – 3 =

2

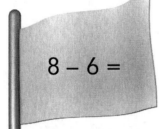
8 – 6 =

4

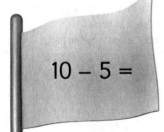
10 – 5 =

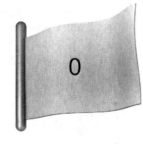
0

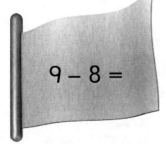
9 – 8 =

5

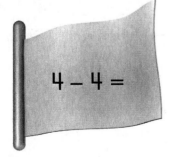
4 – 4 =

1

Stars in Our Flag

Directions: Count the stars on each flag. Then write the number of stars on the line.

1. _____

2. _____

3. _____

4. _____

5. _____

6. _____

Find the Flag

Directions: Help the soldier find his way to the flag.

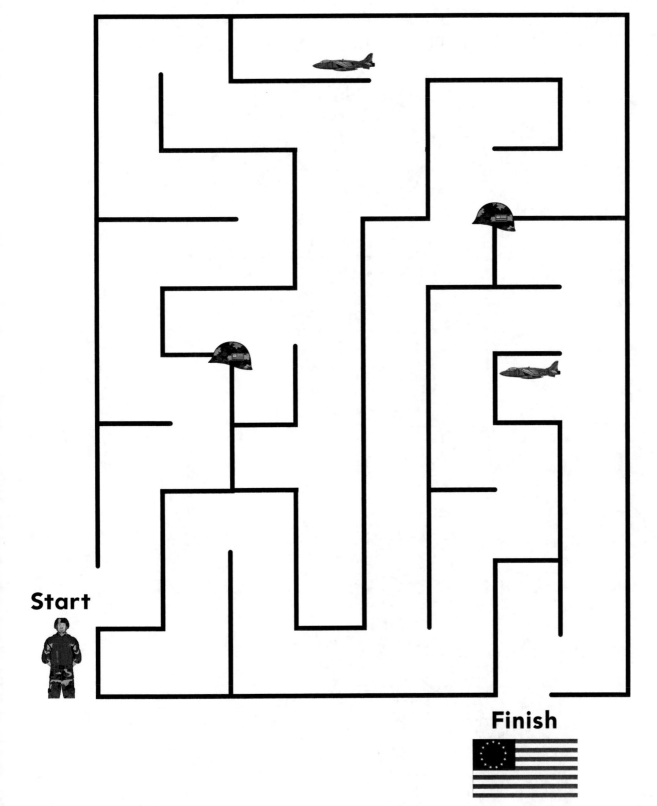

Name _____   Date _____

Design a Uniform

Directions: Soldiers wear many different types of uniforms. Color this the way you would like your uniform to look.

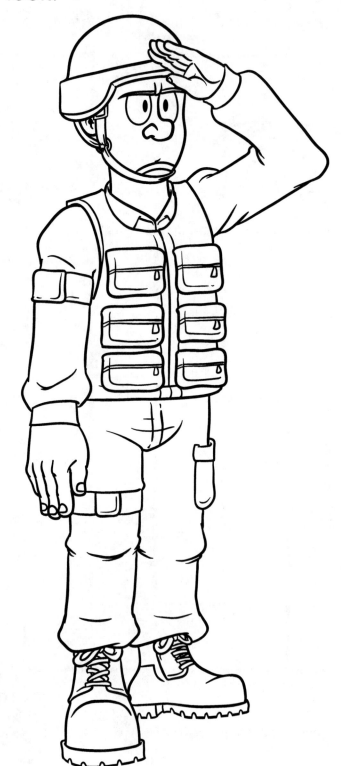

Fireworks Fun

Directions: Create your own fancy fireworks.

Materials

- dark blue or black construction paper
- pencil
- white glue
- glitter in various colors

Steps

1. Draw bursts of fireworks on the paper with the pencil.

2. When you are happy with your design, trace over the burst at the top with glue.

3. Pour glitter onto the wet glue. Pour the excess back into the container. Let it dry.

4. Choose another burst. Trace it with glue. Pour glitter on it.

5. Continue until your creation is finished.

Labor Day
First Monday in September

Background Information

When Labor Day was established in the late 19th century, there was an element of militancy about it. The labor movement, which began more than 100 years before the first Labor Day, grew as the need to protect the interests of workers grew. Trade unions were founded in the late 1700s. The leaders fought for better wages, safe working conditions, and reasonable hours. The labor movement also sought to eliminate child labor and to establish health benefits for workers.

The Knights of Labor was established in 1869. One leader, Peter J. McGuire, suggested to the Central Labor Union of New York City that a day to honor workers be established. (Historians have later suggested that Matthew Maguire may have been the founder of Labor Day. Both men were active in the labor movement.) The first Labor Day parade was held on September 5, 1882. Approximately 10,000 workers marched in the parade, with the Knights of Labor reviewing them. Fireworks, picnics, dancing, and speeches followed. The event was repeated the following year,

and in 1884, the Knights of Labor passed a resolution to make the event permanent. According to McGuire, the choice of date was not significant except that it provided a good break between Independence Day and Thanksgiving.

Oregon was the first state to officially adopt Labor Day in 1887. President Grover Cleveland made the day legal in the District of Columbia in 1894. By 1928, only the state of Wyoming did not celebrate Labor Day. Now, it is observed in the entire United States.

The appreciation for celebrating the unofficial close of summer has increased. Many people have one last vacation over the weekend. For many, Labor Day is truly a day of rest, not labor.

Around the World

Canada has celebrated Labor Day on the first Monday in September since the 1880s. Cuba, Jamaica, India, Malaysia, Norway, the Philippines, and many countries in the Middle East celebrate it in May.

Recommended Books

Bredeson, Carmen. 2001. *Labor Day.* New York: Scholastic.

Osborne, Mary Pope. 1991. *American Tall Tales.* New York: Alfred A. Knopf.

Perez, L. King. 2002. *First Day in Grapes.* New York: Lee and Low.

Name _____   Date _____

Helpful Workers

Directions: Use the Word Bank to solve the Labor Day riddles below.

> **Word Bank**
>
> chef   doctor   farmer   teacher

1.    This person makes good food.

Who is it?

____ ____ ____ ____

- - - - - - - - - - - - - - - - -

____ ____ ____ ____

2.    This person grows the food we eat.

Who is it?

____ ____ ____ ____ ____ ____

- -

____ ____ ____ ____ ____ ____

3.    This person helps keep you well.

Who is it?

____ ____ ____ ____ ____ ____

- -

____ ____ ____ ____ ____ ____

Name _____   **Date** _____

Animals at Work

Directions: Use the words in the Word Bank to help you unscramble the words below.

Word Bank

mule	dog	horse	pig

1.

ogd   ___ ___ ___

2.

elum   ___ ___ ___ ___

3.

orehs   ___ ___ ___ ___ ___

4.

gip   ___ ___ ___

Name _____   Date _____

Connect the Leaves

Directions: Match each addition problem on the left to its answer on the right.

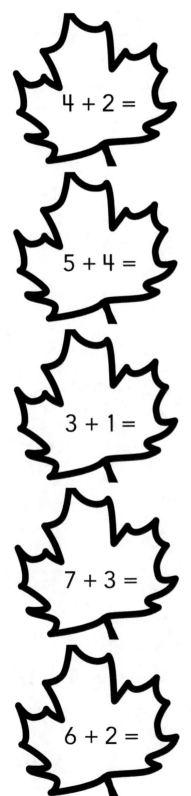

4 + 2 =

5 + 4 =

3 + 1 =

7 + 3 =

6 + 2 =

4

6

9

8

10

#51046—The Big Book of Holidays and Cultural Celebrations   **173**

Name _____ Date _____

Connect the Workers and Tools

Directions: Match each tool on the left to the correct worker on the right.

dancer

writer

nurse

artist

gardener

#51046—The Big Book of Holidays and Cultural Celebrations · © Shell Education

Name _____   Date _____

Labor Day Line Up!

Directions: Put the workers below in alphabetical order.

Word Bank

mailmen	cooks	pilots
nurses	trainers	builders

1. _____

2. _____

3. _____

4. _____

5. _____

6. _____

Name _____   Date _____

Look Again Labor Day!

Directions: These pictures look a lot alike. Circle the 5 differences in the group below.

Back-to-School Bookmarks

Directions: Labor Day means back to school. Make reading even more fun with this bookmark.

Materials

- *Leaves Template* (page 178)
- 1 craft stick
- construction paper in fall colors
- markers
- extra strength glue
- scissors
- pencil

Steps

1. Copy the *Leaves Template* onto various colors of construction paper. Make two of the same pattern. Cut them out.

2. Decorate the paper with markers.

3. Glue a craft stick to the back of one leaf. Glue the matching leaf on the other side of the craft stick.

4. Decorate the craft stick.

5. Make different bookmarks. Keep them in a pencil jar until you need them.

Leaves Template

Rosh Hashanah
1st and 2nd Days of Tishri (September–October)

Yom Kippur
Sunset on the 9th Day to Sunset on the 10th Day of Tishrei (September–October)

Background Information

Rosh Hashanah means "Head of the Year" in Hebrew. In ancient times, the Jewish calendar had four beginnings of the year, each related to the agricultural cycle. Over time, the first day of Tishri (TISH-ri) became the primary observation, perhaps because of the importance of Yom Kippur, also known as the Day of Atonement, and of Sukkot (SOOK-uh), the Feast of Booths (or Tabernacles or Ingathering). Rosh Hashanah is also the time when all are judged for their sins.

The night before Rosh Hashanah, families enjoy a festive meal. The service in the *synagogue* (SIN-uh-gog) on the following day includes meditations, prayer-poems, and readings. Considered New Year's morning, an important ritual is the blowing of the *shofar* (SHOH-fer), made from a ram's horn. During the afternoon of the first day of Rosh Hashanah (unless it falls on the Sabbath), a ceremony by a body of water follows for some Jews. Called *Tashlikh* (tashsh-LEEKH), the ritual involves shaking out one's pockets to symbolize the casting away of sins.

Symbolic foods are eaten during Rosh Hashanah. On the second day, a seasonal fruit is presented, along with a blessing. After a ritual called *washing for bread,* challah (KHAH-luh) bread is raised. Challah and apples are then cut and dipped in honey. A pomegranate is eaten, symbolizing the hope of a sweet year.

Rosh Hashanah also signals 10 days of penitence, ending at Yom Kippur. The night before Yom Kippur, people have a festive meal, including a honey cake. During Yom Kippur, observers fast and focus on repentance. Called the *Day of Atonement*, the evening synagogue service includes prayers and poems. Yom Kippur is considered the most holy day and combines prayer, ritual, memories, poetry, music, and stories from the past. Although solemn, there is an element of joy in recognition of the forgiveness of sins. People ask forgiveness not only from God but also from individuals they have wronged. The shofar signals the start of evening prayers and the end of Yom Kippur. The fast is over.

Recommended Book

Fishman, Cathy Goldberg. 2000. *On Rosh Hashanah and Yom Kippur.* New York: Aladdin.

Name _____   Date _____

Rosh Hashanah and Yom Kippur Riddles

Directions: Use the Word Bank to solve the Rosh Hashanah riddles below.

Word Bank

apple	pray	shofar	Tishri

1. People dip this fruit in honey.

   What is it?

   ___ ___ ___ ___ ___

   -

   ___ ___ ___ ___ ___

2.  Someone blows this on holy days.

   What is it?

   ___ ___ ___ ___ ___ ___

   -

   ___ ___ ___ ___ ___ ___

3.  People do this on holy days.

   What is it?

   ___ ___ ___ ___

   - - - - - - - - - - - - - - - - -

   ___ ___ ___ ___

Name _____   Date _____

Yom Kippur Mixed-Up Words

Directions: Use the Word Bank to unscramble the words below.

Word Bank

cake   candles   sing   pray

1.

_____ _____ _____ _____ _____ _____ _____ _____

- -

_____ _____ _____ _____ _____ _____ _____ _____

andcles

2.

_____ _____ _____ _____

- - - - - - - - - - - -

_____ _____ _____ _____

aypr

3.

_____ _____ _____ _____

- - - - - - - - - - - -

_____ _____ _____ _____

gisn

4.

_____ _____ _____ _____

- - - - - - - - - - - -

_____ _____ _____ _____

kace

Connect the Rosh Hashanah and Yom Kippur Words

Directions: Draw a line to match the Rosh Hashanah and Yom Kippur word parts. Use the pictures to help you.

sho

can

read

hon

ap

far

dles

ey

ing

ple

Name _____ **Date** _____

Yom Kippur Message

Directions: Use the symbols to decode the Yom Kippur message below.

A	B	C	D	E	F	G	H	I	J	K	L	M
*	?	@	#	$	%	^	&	+	=	~	!	>

N	O	P	Q	R	S	T	U	V	W	X	Y	Z
¢	©	∧	÷	∥	±			∩	∞	Σ	Δ	Π	¬

_____ _____ _____ _____   _____ _____
  | &   +   ±   +   ±

_____ _____ _____   _____ _____ _____   _____ _____
 | & $ #   *   Π | ©

_____ _____ _____ _____ _____ _____ _____
 %   © || ^   +   ∞ $

#51046—The Big Book of Holidays and Cultural Celebrations **183**

Connect the Shofars

Directions: Match each addition problem on the left to its answer on the right.

8 + 3 =

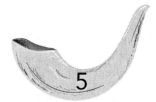

5

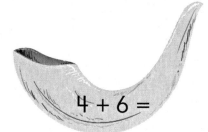

4 + 6 =

11

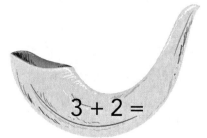

3 + 2 =

9

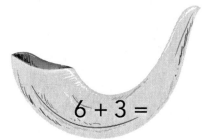

6 + 3 =

10

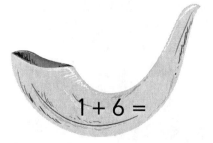

1 + 6 =

7

Look Again Rosh Hashanah!

Directions: These pictures look a lot alike. Circle the 5 differences on the picture on the bottom.

Rosh Hashanah Card

Directions: Make a greeting card for Rosh Hashanah.

Materials

- half an apple
- fork
- paint for the print making
- shallow dish
- scrap paper
- white construction paper
- green marker

Steps

1. Fold the paper in half to make a card.

2. Dip the flat part of the apple into the paint with a fork. Print the apple outline onto the scrap paper. When you are happy with the results open up the card to print on the front and back.

3. Add leaves with a green marker.

4. Let the card dry thoroughly.

5. Write a Happy New Year message inside the card.

Columbus Day
October 12th

Background Information

Christopher Columbus's father was a wool weaver, and he seemed destined to follow that path. However, at age 14, sailors' stories of the sea proved to be too strong an attraction to resist. Trade and new lands were increasingly important to various European countries, and Columbus assumed that the Indies could be reach by crossing the Atlantic Ocean. His request for having a journey funded was rejected by Portugal's John II, England's Henry VII, and the city of Genoa, Italy, his place of birth. King Ferdinand and Queen Isabella of Spain agreed to fund the voyage, although it took a year to work out the arrangements.

Columbus left with the *Santa Maria, Pinta,* and *Niña* on August 3, 1492. After a stop at the Canary Islands for repairs, they left again on September 6. The long journey and poor conditions led the men to near mutiny over the course of the next several weeks. In early October, the men changed course to follow some birds. On October 11, they thought they saw a light, but it wasn't until the next morning that they knew they were approaching land.

Columbus named the land San Salvador, now thought to be one of the islands in the Bahamas. He claimed the land for Spain and called the people *Indians,* thinking that he had landed in India. As he continued on his journey, he landed in Cuba, assuming he was in Japan. While sailing through the various islands in search of wealth, the *Santa Maria* ran aground on a coral reef near Haiti. Thirty-nine men chose to stay behind, while Columbus left for Spain on January 4, 1493.

Columbus sailed west again on September 23, 1893. This time, he had more ships and men. He began to make enemies, however and was charged with cruelty to the men. Although his wealth grew, his health was poor. He died in 1506 without realizing that he had not made it to Asia. Rather, he had come upon a new world that eventually was named after Amerigo Vespucci, another Italian explorer. The first celebration of Columbus Day was on October 12, 1792, in New York City. President Franklin Delano Roosevelt made it a legal holiday for the nation in 1934.

Recommended Books

Aloian, Molly. 2010. *Columbus Day.* New York: Crabtree.

Gardeski, Christina Mia. 2001. *Columbus Day.* New York: Children's Press.

Krensky, Stephen. 1991. *Christopher Columbus.* New York: Random House.

Columbus Day Riddles

Directions: Use the Word Bank to solve the Columbus Day riddles below.

Word Bank

ocean   sail   ship   Spain

1.

This is an object Columbus used to sail.

What is it?

___ ___ ___ ___

- - - - - - - - - - - - - - - - - -

___ ___ ___ ___

2.

He sailed from this country.

What is it?

___ ___ ___ ___ ___

- - - - - - - - - - - - - - - - - -

___ ___ ___ ___ ___

3.

The ship was on this as Columbus was sailing.

What is it?

___ ___ ___ ___ ___

- - - - - - - - - - - - - - - - - -

___ ___ ___ ___ ___

Name _____ **Date** _____

Sailing Away!

Directions: Use the Word Bank to unscramble the words below.

Word Bank
clouds   sun   bird   ship

1.

ousdcl _____

2.

drib _____

3.

hips _____

4.

nus _____

#51046—The Big Book of Holidays and Cultural Celebrations **189**

Name _____ **Date** _____

Look Again Columbus Day!

Directions: These pictures look a lot alike. Circle the 5 differences on the picture on the bottom.

The Santa Maria

Directions: Christopher Columbus had three ships. The main ship was the Santa Maria. Follow the directions and color it.

- Color the main ship brown.
- Leave the sails white.

- Color the waves dark blue.
- Color the sky light blue.

Help Columbus!

Directions: Help Columbus find his ship.

Finish

Start

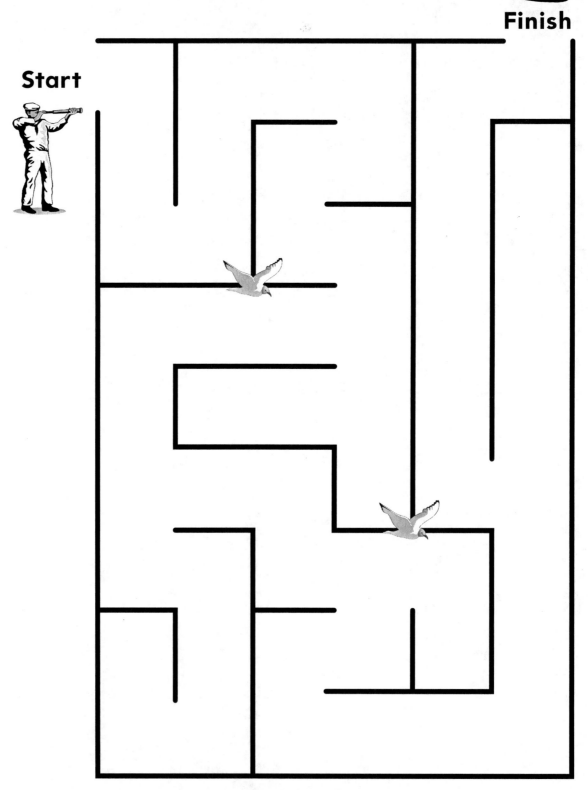

Name _____ **Date** _____

Bon Voyage!

Directions: Give each student one line to read. Have everyone read the last line together.

Reader 1: Christopher Columbus liked the sea.

Reader 2: He loved to sail, but he wanted more.

Reader 3: He asked the queen to pay for a trip.

Reader 4: He got three ships so he could explore.

Reader 5: Before very long, they were on the ships.

Reader 6: They sailed off in search of some land.

Reader 7: They hoped they'd find gold so they could be rich.

Reader 8: Soon they found Cuba, which they thought was Japan.

Reader 9: Christopher Columbus was not ready to quit.

Reader 10: He made other journeys. He got other ships.

Reader 11: He got very rich. But he never knew.

Reader 12: He'd found a New World on that very first trip.

Reader 13: Thank you Columbus.

Reader 14: We want to say,

Reader 15: Have a Happy

Everyone: Columbus Day!

Sail Away with Columbus!

Directions: Make your own ship.

Materials

- clay
- 1 toothpick for each ship
- 1 small square of white paper for each ship
- markers
- glue
- scissors
- brown paint

Steps

1. Cut out a small square sheet of paper. Decorate it with markers.
2. Glue the sail onto the toothpick, or poke the toothpick through the sail.
3. Use your thumb to mold a small ball of clay to make the main ship. Paint it brown.
4. Stick the sail in the clay.

Diwali
Five Days in the Fall

Background Information

Diwali (dee-WAH-lee), the festival of lights, is a Hindu celebration that marks the end of the harvest season and the beginning of the New Year. Celebrated for five continuous days, it is the most important holiday of the year. The exact timing depends on the position of the moon, with the "no moon day" in the month of Kartik (kahr-TEEK) considered the perfect day for Diwali. The main event is the festival of lights. Diwali is a symbol of the victory of good over evil, light over darkness, and truth over falsehood.

On the first day of Diwali, people clean and decorate their homes. Then, people prepare their lamps. In Sanskrit, *Diwali* means "row of lamps." Small earthen oil lamps, called *diyas* (dee-yahz), are lit during Diwali to drive away darkness. Diyas can be simple or ornate. They are displayed inside the home and garden, on outer walls, and on the roof. This practice has its roots in an ancient story. Lord Rama, a king who was exiled by his father, returned. The people celebrated with candles and lights. A newer yet increasingly enjoyable aspect of Diwali is the display of fireworks that fill the sky.

But this festival is about more than lighting diyas. Families and friends gather for special foods and socialization. The story goes that Lakshmi (LUHKSH-mee), the goddess of wealth and prosperity, wanders the Earth looking for homes where she will be welcomed. Hindus welcome her by drawing small footprints with rice flour and vermilion powder on the floor. Celebrants offer sweets to the goddess and sing traditional songs.

Diwali is the most significant time for giving gifts. This demonstrates love, respect, and good wishes for loved ones. Gift giving has broadened to include neighbors, colleagues, and business associates. Gifts may include sweets, dry fruits, jewelry, artifacts, and coins. Celebrants also show respect with prayers of appreciation for prosperity. Each day of Diwali includes the telling of a myth or a legend about a famous god or a goddess.

Recommended Books

Gilmore, Rachna. 2000. *Lights for Gita*. Gardiner, ME: Tilbury House.

Bajaj, Varsha. 2011. *T Is for Taj Mahal: An India Alphabet*. Ann Arbor, MI: Sleeping Bear Press.

Diwali Riddles

Directions: Use the Word Bank to solve the Diwali riddles below.

Word Bank

| clean | diya | gifts | clothes |

1. People buy these for the new year.

   What are they?

   ___ ___ ___ ___ ___ ___ ___

   -

   ___ ___ ___ ___ ___

2. People give these during Diwali.

   What are they?

   ___ ___ ___ ___ ___

   -

   ___ ___ ___ ___ ___

3. People do this to get ready for Diwali.

   What is it?

   ___ ___ ___ ___ ___

   -

   ___ ___ ___ ___ ___

Name _____ **Date** _____

Diwali Fun

Directions: Use the Word Bank to unscramble the Diwali words below.

Word Bank

candle   lamp   star   diya

1.

yaid _____

2.

aecnld _____

3.

trsa _____

4.

palm _____

Animals in India
Word Search

Directions: Find and circle the words in the Word Bank hidden in the puzzle.

Word Bank

anteater	flying fox	rhinoceros
elephant	leopard	tiger

r	h	i	n	o	c	e	r	o	s
h	c	e	s	v	a	l	x	s	v
a	n	t	e	a	t	e	r	o	n
y	t	i	r	w	e	p	v	l	k
d	s	g	s	c	f	h	b	m	l
f	g	e	m	a	c	a	q	u	e
w	e	r	i	u	a	n	r	x	b
x	z	b	e	d	s	t	y	d	s
f	l	y	i	n	g	f	o	x	f
e	l	e	o	p	a	r	d	b	s

Find the Wealth

Directions: Help the footprints find their way to the home.

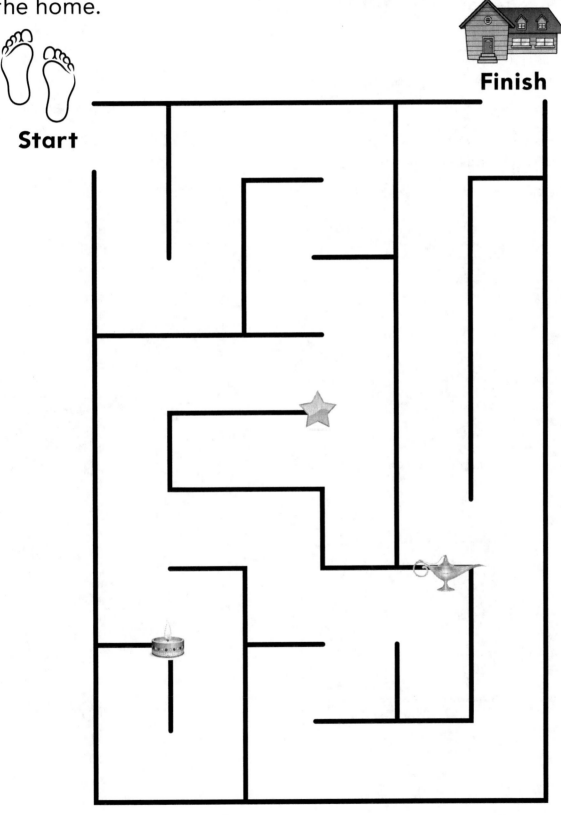

Start

Finish

Diwali

Connect the Oil Lamps

Directions: Match each subtraction problem on the left to its answer on the right.

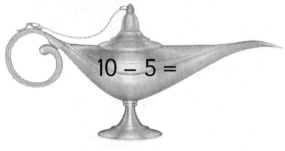

10 – 5 =

6

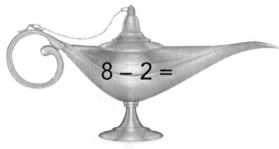

8 – 2 =

1

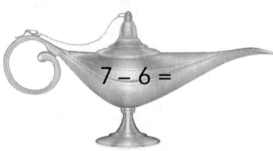

7 – 6 =

5

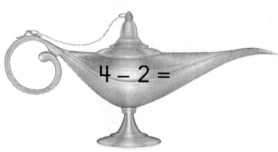

4 – 2 =

3

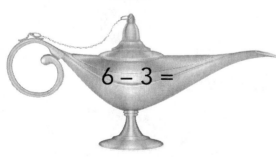

6 – 3 =

2

Name _____   Date _____

Diwali Is Here!

Directions: Give each student one line to read. Have everyone read the last line together.

Reader 1: For five days in the fall,

Reader 2: Diwali is here.

Reader 3: Family and friends

Reader 4: Welcome in the New Year.

Reader 5: We clean up our homes.

Reader 6: We make it all neat.

Reader 7: We bring in good food.

Reader 8: Much of it is sweet.

Reader 9: We listen to stories.

Reader 10: Each one tells a tale

Reader 11: Of gods and goddesses

Reader 12: Who never fail.

Reader 13: Welcome to the New Year!

Reader 14: We want to say,

Reader 15: Have a happy year

Everyone: And a very sweet day!

Diwali Diya

Directions: Make a *diya* for Diwali.

Materials

- air-dry clay

- acrylic paint in brown, orange, yellow, or green

- tea-light candle (optional)

Steps

1. Roll the clay into a ball. Be sure it's big enough to hold the candle when finished.

2. Use your thumbs to shape the clay into a bowl. The tealight candle should fit into it. But it should not be too deep, or the flame will not show. Use the picture as a guide.

3. Let the bowl air-dry, or bake it.

4. Paint the dry bowl with colors such as brown, orange, yellow, or green.

5. Let the paint dry.

6. Place the tea-light candle in the bowl when ready to use. Have your family light it at home.

Halloween
October 31st
Day of the Dead
November 1st-2nd

Halloween Background

Halloween means "the evening before All Hallows or All Saints' Day." The day traces back to the Celtics in Wales, Ireland, Brittany, and the Highlands of Scotland, who followed the leadership of a clergy. This group of spiritual people included healers and leaders, who were in tune with nature. This time of year was considered the new year. The harvests were done, and the year was beginning again.

November 1 was the day that cattle were returned to the barns for the winter. The Celtic people believed that the dead returned to be among the living at this point. Samhain, the Lord of the Dead, judged the souls. The sinful were likely to be sent to live in the bodies of animals. Some people wore masks and costumes as they tried to lead the ghosts away from the feast in a parade. Ritual sacrifices were held with criminals, horses, and black cats being burned to death. Fires were important during Halloween, with various purposes: to replenish the sun for purification, for reading the future, and to scare away the evil spirits.

Day of the Dead Background

This primarily Mexican holiday reflects the ancient practices of gathering to remember family and loved ones who have died. Children are honored on November 1, *Dia de los Inocentes* (DEE-yah deh lohs in-oh-SEN-tez) or *Dia de los Angelitos* (DEE-yah deh lohs ahn-hey-LEE-toz), with the Day of the Dead, *Dia de los Muertos* (DEE-yah deh lohs mwhehr-toz), following on November 2. Indigenous cultures honored the dead with rituals and artifacts such as skulls. During ancient times, the monthlong activities came during the ninth month of the Aztec solar calendar, usually late summer. When the Spaniards came to Mexico, they considered the rituals to be sacrilegious and moved the celebration date to coincide with All Saints Day (November 1) and All Souls Day (November 2). Currently, celebrations vary. Many people go to cemeteries. They build altars and bring food, beverages, small gifts, and memorabilia. Graves are cleaned and decorated. Some people wear masks and dance in honor of the dead.

Recommended Books

Landau, Elaine. 2011. *What Is Halloween?* Berkeley Heights, NJ: Enslow.

Duval, Kathy. 2007. *The Three Bears' Halloween*. New York: Holiday House.

Goldman, Judy. 2008. *Uncle Monarch and the Day of the Dead*. Honesdale, PA: Boyds Mill Press.

Name _____   Date _____

Halloween Fun!

Directions: Use the Word Bank to solve the Halloween riddles below.

Word Bank

apples   black cat   ghost   mask

1.  Some people think this is bad luck.

   What is it?

   ____ ____ ____ ____ ____ ____   ____ ____ ____
   - - - - - - - - - - - - - - - - - -   - - - - - - - - -
   ____ ____ ____ ____ ____ ____   ____ ____ ____

2. This says "Boo!"

   What is it?

   ____ ____ ____ ____ ____
   - - - - - - - - - - - - - - - - - -
   ____ ____ ____ ____ ____

3. You might wear this on your face.

   What is it?

   ____ ____ ____ ____
   - - - - - - - - - - - - - - - -
   ____ ____ ____ ____

 #51046—The Big Book of Holidays and Cultural Celebrations

Name _____   Date _____

Mixed-up Halloween Words

Directions: Use the Word Bank to unscramble the Halloween words below.

Word Bank

bat   cat   spider   ghost

1.

   __ __ __ __ __

   _ _ _ _ _ _ _ _ _ _ _ _ _

   __ __ __ __ __

   gohts

2.

   __ __ __

   _ _ _ _ _ _ _ _

   __ __ __

   act

3.

   __ __ __ __ __ __

   _ _ _ _ _ _ _ _ _ _ _ _ _

   __ __ __ __ __ __

   despri

4.

   __ __ __

   _ _ _ _ _ _ _ _

   __ __ __

   tab

Name _____   Date _____

Connect the Halloween Costumes

Directions: Draw a line to match the Halloween costume word parts. Use the pictures to help you.

astro   **naut**

lady   **on**

drag   **bug**

qu   **bot**

ro   **een**

Name _____ **Date** _____

Halloween Safety

Directions: Use the symbols to decode the Halloween message below.

A	B	C	D	E	F	G	H	I	J	K	L	M
*	?	@	#	$	%	^	&	+	=	~	!	>

N	O	P	Q	R	S	T	U	V	W	X	Y	Z
¢	©	∧	÷	‖	±			∩	∞	Σ	Δ	Π	¬

___ ___ ___ ___   ___ ___ ___

&   *   ∞ $ %   ∩   ¢ ,

___ ___ ___   ___ ___ ___ ___

?   ∩ | ± | *   Π

___ ___ ___ ___ .

±   *   % $

Name _____   Date _____

Follow the Grinning Jack-o'-Lanterns!

Directions: Start at the grinning Jack. Draw a line to connect all of the grinning Jacks. Can you get to the treat?

Start

Name _____ Date _____

Five Pumpkins Plus!

Directions: Give each student one line to read. Have everyone read the last line together.

Reader 1:   Five little pumpkins sitting on a gate.

Reader 2:   The first one said, "It's getting late."

Reader 3:   The second one said, "Who goes there?"

Reader 4:   The third one said, "Ghosts are in the air!"

Reader 5:   The fourth one said, "We'd better run!"

Reader 6:   The fifth one said, "But that's no fun!"

Reader 7:   There are lots more pumpkins sitting on the gate.

Reader 8:   The sixth one said, "Let's just wait."

Reader 9:   The seventh one said, "I see a black cat!"

Reader 10: The eighth one said, "I see a black bat!"

Reader 11: The ninth one said, "I think the night is done."

Reader 12: The tenth one said, "It's been lots of fun."

Reader 13: Ten little pumpkins all left the scene.

Everyone: See you next year! Happy Halloween!

Pumpkin Seed Jack-o'-Lantern

Directions: Make your own Jack-o'-Lantern out of pumpkin seeds.

Materials

- pumpkin seeds
- black construction paper
- orange, green, brown, and yellow paint
- paintbrush
- glue

Steps

1. Paint enough pumpkin seeds orange to form a pumpkin.

2. Paint enough pumpkin seeds green to make a leaf.

3. Paint eight pumpkin seeds brown to make a stump.

4. Paint pumpkin seeds yellow to make the eyes, nose, and mouth.

5. Glue the pumpkin seeds on the black construction paper to make a jack-o'-lantern.

Veterans Day
November 11th

Background Information

The United States entered World War I on April 6, 1917. More than 100,000 soldiers were lost in the war. President Woodrow Wilson, upon being asked for an armistice by the Germans, insisted that Kaiser Wilhelm II abdicate his throne in favor of a democracy. The Kaiser abdicated on November 9, and the armistice was signed on November 11. News of the armistice reached the United States early in the morning, prompting the blowing of whistles and sirens. People lit bonfires and celebrated in the streets.

One year later, people celebrated the end of the biggest war to date on the first Armistice Day. Veterans paraded, and people attended church services. At exactly 11:00 A.M., the time of the cease-fire, two minutes of silence were observed in honor of the dead soldiers. Many soldiers had been buried without complete records or identification. Both France and England honored those soldiers by placing the body of one unknown soldier beneath the Arc de Triomphe in Paris on Armistice Day. Another soldier was entombed in Westminster Abbey in London.

The United States followed suit in 1921, placing a soldier in a crypt in Arlington National Cemetery in Arlington, Virginia. The tomb, then called the Tomb of the Unknown Soldier, is guarded at all times. The guard changes every hour on the hour.

Prompted by World War II and the Korean War, many people wanted to honor all of the veterans who had served the country. On June 1, 1954, President Dwight D. Eisenhower signed into law the establishment of Veterans Day. Several years later, unknown soldiers from both World War II and the Korean War joined the World War I Unknown Soldier in Arlington National Cemetery. The site is now called the Tomb of the Unknowns.

Around the World

The British Commonwealth celebrates Remembrance Sunday. Two minutes of silence occur at the 11th hour of the 11th day of the eleventh month, the time when the armistice became effective. Canada has Remembrance Day. France and Australia also honor the losses in both World War I and World War II on or near November 11.

Recommended Books

Catalanotto, Peter and Pamela Schembri. 2008. *The Veterans Day Visitor.* New York: Holt.

Landau, Elaine. 2002. *Veterans Day—Remembering Our War Heroes.* Berkeley Heights, NJ: Enslow.

Veterans Day Riddles

Directions: Use the Word Bank to solve the Veterans Day riddles below.

Word Bank

| jet | jeep | ship | tank |

1. This is used in battles on land.

What is it?

____ ____ ____ ____

- - - - - - - - - - - - - - - - - -

____ ____ ____ ____

2. This can go on rough roads.

What is it?

____ ____ ____ ____

- - - - - - - - - - - - - - - - - -

____ ____ ____ ____

3. This flies high and fast.

What is it?

____ ____ ____

- - - - - - - - - - - - - -

____ ____ ____

Getting Dressed

Directions: Use the Word Bank to unscramble the clothing items below.

Word Bank

boots   helmet   shirt   socks

1.

rthis

_____
- - - - - - - - - - - - - - - - - - - -
_____

2.

ssokc

_____
- - - - - - - - - - - - - - - - - - - -
_____

3.

botos

_____
- - - - - - - - - - - - - - - - - - - -
_____

4.

methel

_____
- - - - - - - - - - - - - - - - - - - -
_____

Veterans Day

At Your Service

Directions: Match each worker on the left to their correct job title on the right.

firefighter

soldier

nurse

chef

librarian

#51046—*The Big Book of Holidays and Cultural Celebrations*

Look Again Veterans Day!

Directions: These pictures look a lot alike. Circle the 5 differences on the jeep on the bottom.

Name _____   Date _____

Follow the Camouflage!

Directions: Start at the camouflage helmet. Draw a line to connect all of the camouflage helmets. Can you get to the jeep?

Start

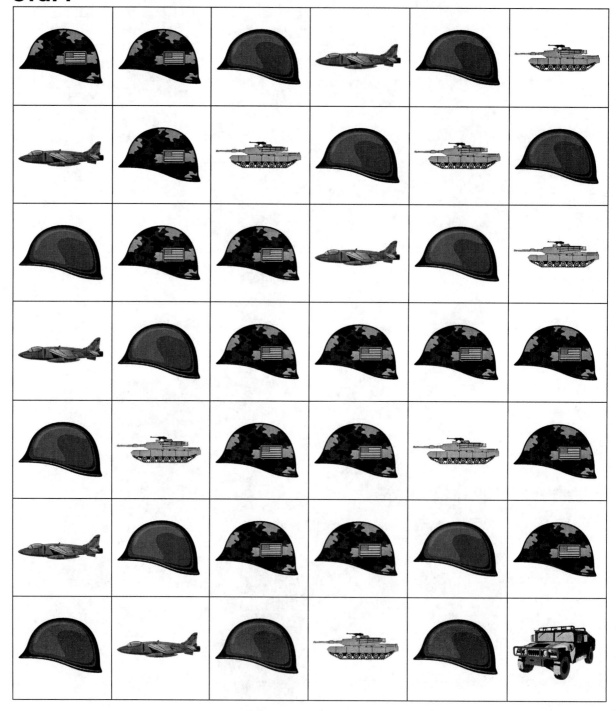

Name _____   Date _____

Veterans Day

Directions: Give each student one line to read. Have everyone read the last line together.

Reader 1:   The first Armistice Day was for World War I.

Reader 2:   An *armistice* means that the fighting is done.

Reader 3:   The fighting had stopped on this very day.

Reader 4:   The battle was over. Our soldiers had won.

Reader 5:   Armistice Day changed to Veterans Day.

Reader 6:   The change came in 1954.

Reader 7:   America wanted to honor all vets

Reader 8:   At home or away in war.

Reader 9:   The Tomb of the Unknowns holds soldiers.

Reader 10: It helps honor those who have died.

Reader 11: We have parades and remember those people

Reader 12: Who served as protectors with pride.

Reader 13: Thank you to the soldiers.

Reader 14: We all wish war would cease.

Reader 15: Thank you for your service

Everyone: In helping work for peace.

Camouflage Prints

Directions: Soldiers wear camouflage so they can hide easily. Make your own camouflage prints.

Materials

- large sheet of white construction paper

- sponges

- paint in camouflage colors, such as brown, beige, and green

- shallow dishes for the paints

Steps

1. Decide the colors you want to use. For a jungle, use mostly green colors. For a desert, use mostly brown colors.

2. Dip a sponge in one color. Make splotches around the paper.

3. Dip a sponge in another color. Make more splotches.

4. Keep adding colors and splotches. You can leave a few areas white.

5. Let the paper dry.

6. Write a message to a soldier on the back.

Thanksgiving
Fourth Thursday in November

Background Information

When the Pilgrims left England for Holland because of religious persecution, they found that they were not well suited to an urban setting. They struggled with the language and were unprepared to work in the various trades that were their options. They voted to go to America, with the tobacco industry serving as an important attraction. The Pilgrims were split between the *Mayflower* and the *Speedwell,* but repairs to the *Speedwell* delayed them twice. On September 6, 1620, 102 people left for America.

William Butten, a servant, died on the voyage. On November 11, the ship anchored at the tip of Cape Cod. Before landing, the Mayflower Compact was drawn up, and John Carver became the first governor. The Pilgrims chose to colonize Plymouth, previously Patuxet, left a ghost town by plague, which had wiped out the Indian population.

Squanto, who had lived in Patuxet, proved to be an important ally and resource for the Pilgrims. Squanto had been captured and sold into slavery in Spain. He escaped to England. Just six months before the Pilgrims landed, he had returned to Patuxet. Squanto helped the Pilgrims build houses that first winter. However, because of a poor diet and a bitter winter, 47 people, including John Carver, died of scurvy and pneumonia. That spring, Squanto helped them plant their first crops and taught them how to fish. The harvest was adequate, prompting the first celebration of thanks. The Wampanoag Indians' chief came, along with 90 braves, bringing deer to add to the feast. Captain Myles Standish paraded the soldiers, the Indians demonstrated their skills, and everyone joined in games of racing and jumping.

George Washington issued the first Thanksgiving proclamation in 1789. However, it was Sarah Josepha Hale who wrote articles and editorials that convinced President Lincoln to establish Thanksgiving as a national holiday in 1863.

Recommended Books

Atwell, Debbie. 2006. *The Thanksgiving Door.* New York: Houghton Mifflin.

Cox, Judy. 2008. *One Is a Feast for Mouse: A Thanksgiving Tale.* New York: Holiday House.

Silvano, Wendi. 2009. *Turkey Trouble.* Tarrytown, NY: Marshall Cavendish.

Name _____   Date _____

Thanksgiving Riddles

Directions: Use the Word Bank to solve the Thanksgiving Day riddles below.

Word Bank

corn	fish	ocean	Pilgrims

1. 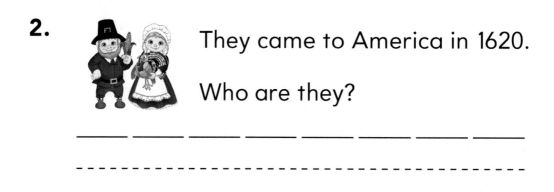 Pilgrims had to learn how to catch these.

   What are they?

   ____ ____ ____ ____

   -

   ____ ____ ____ ____

2. They came to America in 1620.

   Who are they?

   ____ ____ ____ ____ ____ ____ ____ ____

   -

   ____ ____ ____ ____ ____ ____ ____ ____

3. American Indians taught the Pilgrims to grow this.

   What is it?

   ____ ____ ____ ____

   - - - - - - - - - - - - - - - - - - -

   ____ ____ ____ ____

Name _____   **Date** _____

The Menu

Directions: Use the Word Bank to unscramble the menu words below.

Word Bank

corn   duck   fish   grapes

1.

kduc _____

- -

_____

2.

shif _____

- -

_____

3.

rocn _____

- -

_____

4.

praesg _____

- -

_____

Name _____   Date _____

Connect the Feast

Directions: Draw a line to match the Thanksgiving food word parts. Use the pictures to help you.

tur

tato

cran

key

sweet po

berries

pump

kin

Name _____   Date _____

Dressing as a Pilgrim

Directions: Use the Word Bank to help you label the Pilgrim's clothing.

Word Bank

cuffs: worn on the wrist
doublet: worn like a jacket
hat: worn on the head
ruff: worn around the neck
shoes: worn on the feet

_____

_____

_____

_____

_____

_____

_____

_____

_____

Name _____   **Date** _____

Thanksgiving Cinquain

Directions: Create a poem for Thanksgiving.

G
I
V
E
T
H
A
N
K
S

Name _____ Date _____

Tom Turkey's Thanksgiving

Directions: Give each student one line to read. Have everyone read the last line together.

Reader 1: Tom Turkey woke one morning.

Reader 2: The duck and the goose looked sad.

Reader 3: "What's the matter?" said Tom.

Reader 4: "Has something happened that's bad?"

Reader 5: "Tomorrow is Thanksgiving,"

Reader 6: The duck and the goose both cried.

Reader 7: "The dinner will be turkey!

Reader 8: We think that you should hide!

Reader 9: "What shall I do?" asked Tom.

Reader 10: Tom had tears in his eyes.

Reader 11: "I have an idea," said Duck.

Reader 12: "We just need a disguise.

Reader 13: We can get help from Miss Hen."

Reader 14: Soon the farmer came outside.

Reader 15 What do you think he saw?

Reader 16: The duck was covered with mud.

Reader 17: Tom Turkey was covered with straw.

Reader 18: The hen had five turkey feathers

Reader 19: Sticking out of her tail.

Reader 20: The goose said, "Quack, quack, quack,"

Reader 21: And jumped up on a pail.

Reader 22: The farmer laughed and said,

Reader 23: "Tom Turkey has nothing to fear.

Reader 24: We'll all have a Happy Thanksgiving.

Reader 25: We'll eat veggie burgers this year!"

Everyone: Happy Thanksgiving!

Turkey Mosaic

Directions: Create a *hand*some turkey mosaic.

Materials

- paper plate
- mosaic materials (dried beans, peas, pasta) in fall colors
- pencil
- glue

Steps

1. Place your hand on the paper plate. Spread out your fingers.
2. Trace around your hand, or have a friend help you. This is the outline of the turkey. Your thumb is its head.
3. Choose your mosaic materials.
4. Arrange a design to show that it is a turkey.
5. When you are pleased with the design, glue the mosaic materials in place.
6. Display for Thanksgiving.

Hanukkah

Eight Days, beginning on the eve of the 25th Day of the Lunar Month of Kislev

Late November through December

Background Information

Known as the Festival of Lights, Hanukkah is marked by the burning of candles in the nine-branched *menorah* (muh-NAWR-uh). During the second century B.C., the *books of the Maccabees* described how Palestine had come under the rule of the Syrian king Antiochus III, known as Antiochus III the Great. Antiochus IV began a campaign to Hellenize, or make more Greek-like, the people of Judea. Many of the religious customs of the Jews were ignored or blatantly violated.

A small band of faithful Jews chose to rebel. The partisans prevailed against Antiochus's forces and reclaimed the Temple sanctuary. While reestablishing the traditional order of worship, the Maccabees declared an eight-day ceremony of rededication, beginning on the 25 day of Kislev (KIS-luhv), to be known as Hanukkah. Once the Maccabean partisans prepared to light the sacred lamp in the Temple sanctuary, they discovered that most of the oil for the lamp had been defiled. There was enough pure oil remaining for one day. They lit the lamp, and the oil burned for eight days—the length of time it took to have new oil prepared.

During Hanukkah, people generally light a single candle on the first night, adding another on each of eight subsequent nights. Praise and prayers are offered. Oily foods are eaten, such as *latkes*, pronounced LAHT-kuhs, (potato pancakes), and *sufganiyot* (doughnuts), pronounced sahf-GAN-ee-yoht.

The dreidel (DREYD-I) is a four-sided spinning top. One purported explanation of the connection of the dreidel with Hanukkah dates back to Antiochus's rule, when the Torah schools were banned. Students studied in the forests, and when a patrol approached, the books were hidden and children began playing with dreidels. Today's dreidel has Hebrew letters on the sides that stand for *a great miracle happened there*, referring to the miracle of the oil. Players begin with a stash of coins, markers, or treats. Depending on which side the dreidel falls, each player gains or loses some of his or her stash. Children also receive gifts during Hanukkah, along with a reminder to share with charity.

Recommended Books

Cleary, Brian P. 2006. *Eight Wild Nights: A Family Hanukkah Tale*. MN: Kar-Ben Publishing.

Lehman-Wilzig, Tami and Nicole Katzman. *Nathan Blows Out the Hanukkah Candles*. Inneapolis, MN: Kar-Ben Publishing, 2011.

Name _____   **Date** _____

Hanukkah Riddles

Directions: Use the Word Bank to solve the Hanukkah riddles below.

Word Bank

dreidel   candles   latkes   olives

1.   These are lit up.

What are they?

___ ___ ___ ___ ___ ___ ___

- -

___ ___ ___ ___ ___ ___ ___

2.   These are used to make oil.

What are they?

___ ___ ___ ___ ___ ___

- -

___ ___ ___ ___ ___ ___

3.   Children play with this during Hanukkah.

What is it?

___ ___ ___ ___ ___ ___ ___

- -

___ ___ ___ ___ ___ ___ ___

Name _____   Date _____

Hanukkah Lights

Directions: Use the Word Bank to unscramble the light words below.

```
Word Bank

moon        star        sun        candle
```

1.

nomo   _____
- -
_____

2.

eacndl   _____
- -
_____

3.

tars   _____
- -
_____

4.

uns   _____
- -
_____

Name _____ **Date** _____

Connect the Dreidels

Directions: Match each addition problem on the left to its answer on the right.

3 + 3 =

9

4 + 5 =

6

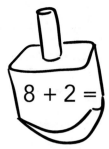
8 + 2 =

7

2 + 5 =

10

1 + 3 =

4

Eight Days of Hanukkah

Directions: A candle is lit each night for eight days. The middle one remains lit. Start with two candles. Then find three. Can you get up to nine? Find the right path.

Start Here:

Name _____   **Date** _____

Make a Dreidel

Directions: Follow the grid to copy the dreidel. Draw each piece in the box with the same number.

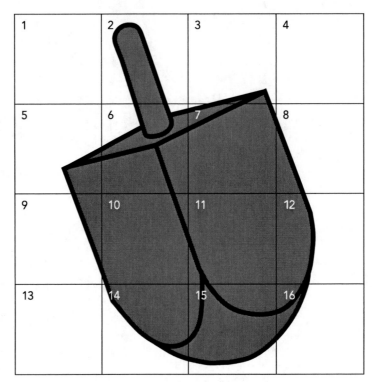

1	2	3	4
5	6	7	8
9	10	11	12
13	14	15	16

Name _____   **Date** _____

Hanukkah Line Up!

Directions: Put the Hanukkah words below in alphabetical order.

Word Bank

dreidel	moon	latkes
sun	lamp	candles

---

1. _____

2. _____

3. _____

4. _____

5. _____

6. _____

Star of David Ornament

Directions: Decorate a Star of David ornament.

Materials

- *Star Template* (page 235)
- pencil
- construction paper
- scissors
- blue or gold paint
- salt
- white yarn
- hole punch

Steps

1. Trace the *Star Template* onto the construction paper.
2. Cut it out.
3. Paint it blue or gold.
4. Sprinkle salt on the paint while it is wet.
5. Let it dry.
6. Punch a hole in one point. String yarn through and hang the star.

Star Template

Kwanzaa
December 26th to January 1st

Background Information

The first Kwanzaa, conceived and developed by Maulana Karenga (born Ronald McKinley Everett), was celebrated in 1966. Dr. Karenga, a professor of African studies, based the holiday on harvest celebrations practiced in parts of Africa. Concerned that African Americans were losing their connections to their African roots, he promoted Kwanzaa as a way to recommit to seven key principles, with an emphasis on the importance of family life: unity, self-determination, collective work and responsibility, cooperative economics, purpose, creativity, and faith. Considered a way of life as much as a celebration, Kwanzaa serves as a way of remembering one's roots, rejoicing in one's life, reassessing and recommitting one's life, and looking to the future.

There are several symbols of Kwanzaa to help focus African Americans during Kwanzaa. The *mkeka* (em-KEH-kah) is a straw or cloth mat upon which the other symbols are placed. The *kinara* (kee-NAH-rah) holds seven candles. The seven candles, *mishumaa* (mee-shoo-MAH-ah), represent the power of the sun, the seven principles, and the colors of the Pan-African flag: black (the color of black people), red (the color of Shango, who is the god of fire, thunder, and lightning, and the blood of ancestors), and green (the harvest of Earth). An ear of corn, *muhindi* (moo-HEEN-dee), represents the children or offspring of the stalk of corn (parents). The *kikombe cha umoja* (kee-KOHM-beh cha oo-MOH-jah) is the Unity Cup, reminding celebrants to honor their ancestors. Gifts, or *zawadi* (zuh-weh-dee), may be presented to remind children of good acts. The feast, *karamu* (kah-RAH-moo), symbolizes the power of celebrating as a community.

Kwanzaa preparations generally involve the entire family, with the symbols gathered by December 19. On December 26, the leader calls the family together and launches the celebration with greetings, prayers, a call for unity, singing, a lighting ceremony, a discussion of the principle of the day, a story, and the optional giving of a gift. Each day follows with an exploration of the related principle. The feast, held on December 31, may also include drumming and dancing.

Recommended Books

McKissack, Lisa Beringer and Fredrick L. McKissack Jr. 2000. *Kwanzaa—Count and Celebrate!* Berkeley Heights, NJ: Enslow.

Medearis, Angela Shelf. 2000. *Seven Spools of Thread: A Kwanzaa Story.* Park Ridge, IL: Albert Whitman.

Name _____   **Date** _____

Kwanzaa Riddles

Directions: Use the Word Bank to solve the Kwanzaa riddles below.

Word Bank

cup   gifts   mat

1.    People drink from this to show unity. That means acting as one.

What is it?

____ ____ ____

- - - - - - - - - - - - - -

____ ____ ____

2.   People give these during Kwanzaa.

What are they?

____ ____ ____ ____ ____

- -

____ ____ ____ ____ ____

3. ⬛   Things for Kwanzaa are put on this.

What is it?

____ ____ ____

- - - - - - - - - - - - - -

____ ____ ____

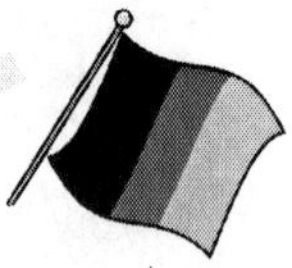

Name _____   **Date** _____

First Fruits

Directions: Use the Word Bank below to unscramble the foods that are eaten during Kwanzaa.

Word Bank			
orange	corn	pear	grapes

1.

ograne _____

2.

sprage _____

3.

earp _____

4.

nocr _____

Name _____ Date _____

Connect the Kwanzaa Words

Directions: Draw a line to match the Kwanzaa word parts. Use the pictures to help you.

kin

dles

uni

ara

can

ty cup

corn

stalk

ap

ple

 #51046—The Big Book of Holidays and Cultural Celebrations

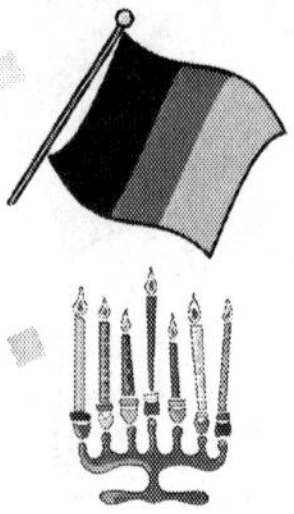

Name _____ Date _____

Connect the Kinaras

Directions: Start at the complete kinara. Draw lines only to the complete kinaras. Can you get to the unity cup?

Start

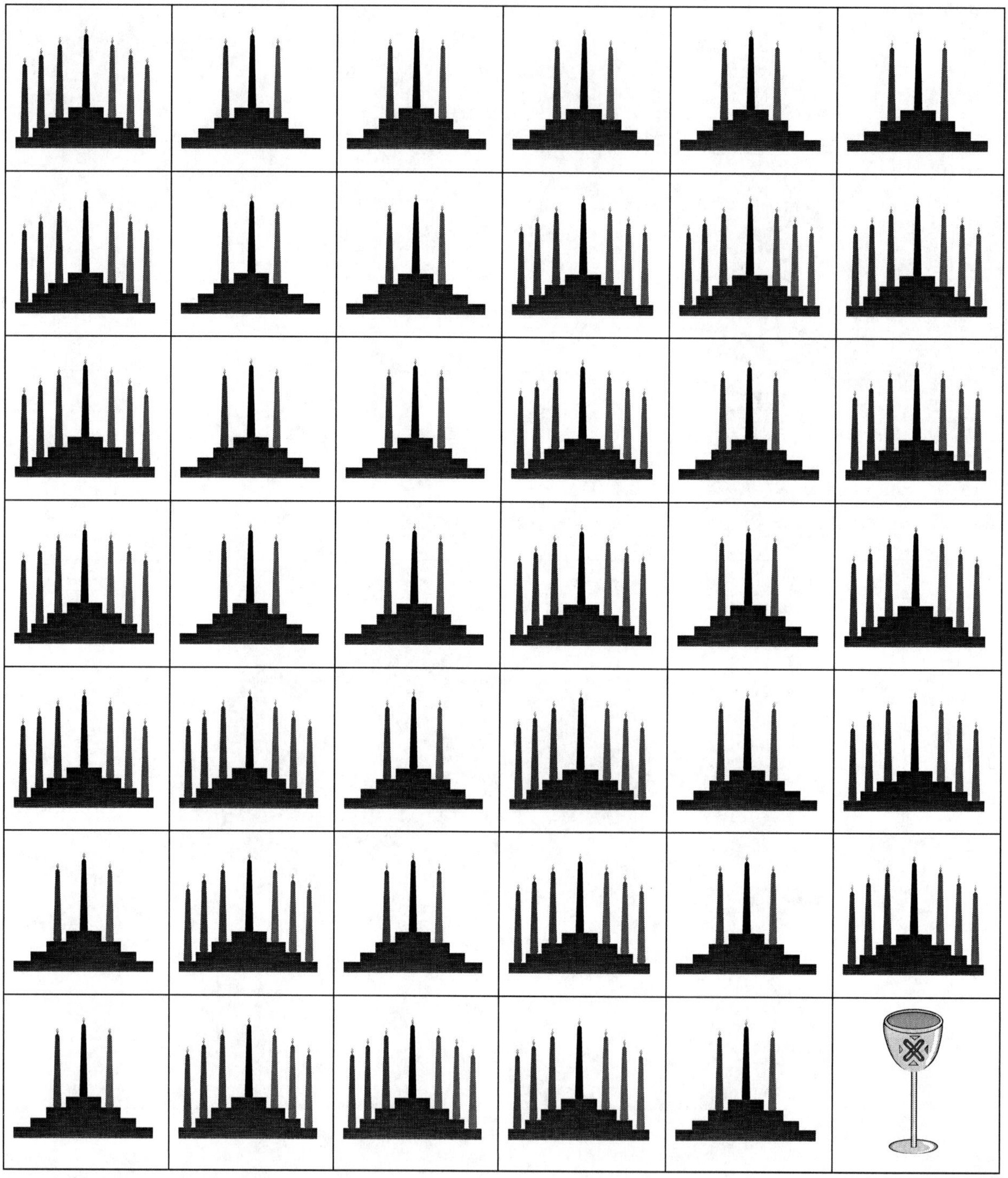

Name _____ **Date** _____

Kwanzaa Harvest

Directions: The fall harvest is important to Kwanzaa. Sort these foods into the right baskets. Write their names on the lines.

Word Bank

apples   bacon   carrots   wheat

Fruit	_____
Vegetable	_____
Grain	_____
Meat	_____

Kwanzaa

Find the Kinara

Directions: Help the candle find its way to the kinara.

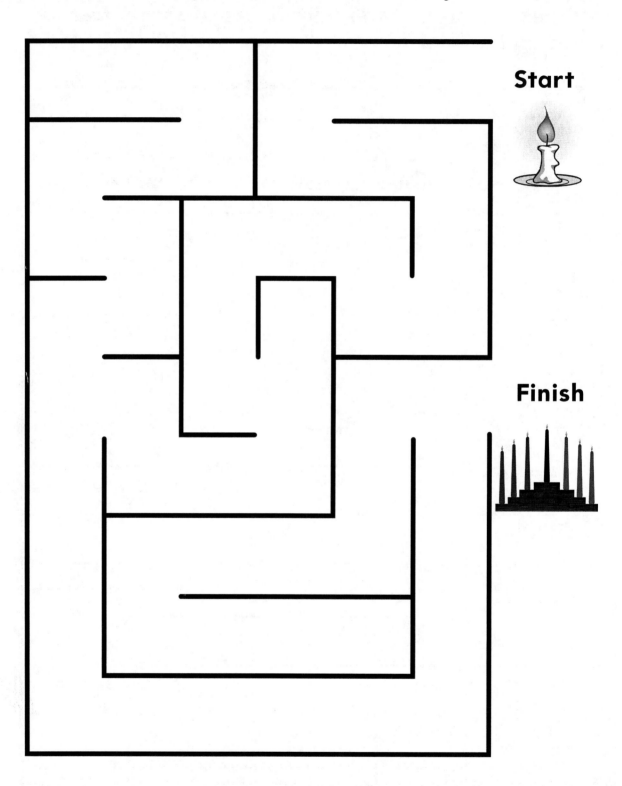

Start

Finish

Kwanzaa Mat

Directions: Make your own *mkeka* (em-keh-kah), a woven mat, for Kwanzaa.

Materials

- black, green, and red construction paper

- scissors

- ruler

- tape or glue

- pencil

Steps

1. Use the ruler to mark one inch across each short end of the paper.

2. Connect the lines. You should have eight lines.

3. Fold the paper in half horizontally.

4. Cut the lines across. Do not cut all the way to the end. Leave one inch uncut. Unfold your paper. This is your base.

5. Measure 1-inch by 9-inch strips of the red and green paper.

6. Cut the strips.

7. Weave each strip into the base. Start with a strip of one color. Then use the other color.

8. Use tape or glue to hold the strips in place.

Christmas
December 25th

Background Information

Christmas celebrates the birth of Jesus Christ, born in Bethlehem to the Virgin Mary and Joseph. Scholars disagree regarding the actual date of the birth of Christ. In the ancient Roman world, December 25 was celebrated as the *Natalis Solis Invicti,* the birthday of the Unconquerable Sun, Mithras. Mithras was so popular among the Romans in the third century that Mithraism became a threat to Christianity. They had much in common, such as the belief in holy water, the shepherds and their gifts, and communion. Over time, the celebration of Christ's birth on December 25 overshadowed the pagan practices of sun worship.

Christmas in the New World began on December 25, 1492. Christopher Columbus's ship, the *Santa Maria,* was caught on a reef off the coast of Haiti. It had to be abandoned, and a fort named La Navidad, or the Nativity, was built of its timber. The Puritans, in contrast, did not believe in celebrating Christmas. Indeed, Massachusetts essentially outlawed observances in 1659, with a five-schilling fine if caught feasting or relaxing.

However, this was repealed by 1681 thanks to the influx of people for whom Christmas was a joyous occasion.

Christmas has been influenced by several cultures. The Germans brought the Christmas tree and Kris Kringle, known as Santa Claus. The French brought the wandering of the Three Kings to New Orleans, along with Papa Noël. The English imported the custom of caroling on Christmas Eve, and many churches today hold caroling services. *Yuletide,* referring to the Christmas season, dates back to a Celtic-German feast at the beginning of November, hinting of Halloween and known as *Yule* in Scandinavia. The festival became a winter solstice celebration, merging with Christmas as Christianity grew. The kindling of the Yule log, a large log of oak, was an important ritual as winter approached. It was put away and protected from year to year after a brief stint on the fire. The Scandinavians also burned candles, representing the divine light. An Irish legend says that candles should be lit in the window to guide Mary and Joseph to a welcoming home.

Recommended Books

Landau, Elaine. 2011. *What Is Christmas?* Berkeley Heights, NJ: Enslow.

Moore, Clement Clarke. 2002. *The Night Before Christmas Pop-Up.* New York: Little Simon.

Name _____ **Date** _____

Christmas Riddles

Directions: Use the Word Bank to solve the Christmas riddles below.

Word Bank

carols	elves	Frosty	Santa

1.  He flies in a sleigh.

Who is he?

___ ___ ___ ___ ___

- -

___ ___ ___ ___ ___

2.  People sing these songs for Christmas.

What are they?

___ ___ ___ ___ ___ ___

- -

___ ___ ___ ___ ___ ___

3. They help Santa make toys.

Who are they?

___ ___ ___ ___ ___

- - - - - - - - - - - - - - - - - - -

___ ___ ___ ___ ___

Name _____ **Date** _____

Decorate the Tree!

Directions: Use the Word Bank to unscramble the Christmas tree words below.

Word Bank

angel   balls   lights   star

1.

nagle   _____
          -
          _____

2.

srta   _____
          -
          _____

3.

lbals   _____
          -
          _____

4.

htlgis   _____
          -
          _____

#51046—The Big Book of Holidays and Cultural Celebrations   © Shell Education

Name _____   Date _____

Get to Work!

Directions: Follow the steps to help Santa's elves collect the letters. Circle them and write them in the blanks to find the hidden message. The first letter is done for you.

1. Walk 5 spaces to the right. Write the letter here. _____ **C** _____

4. Walk 4 spaces to the left. Write the letter here. _____ - - - - - _____

2. Walk 4 spaces to the right. Write the letter here. _____ - - - - - _____

5. Walk 2 spaces to the left. Write the letter here. _____ - - - - - _____

3. Walk 3 spaces down. Write the letter here. _____ - - - - - _____

6. Walk 2 spaces up. Write the letter here. _____ - - - - - _____

Start	a	c	e	i	(c)	p	u	f	a
c	k	r	s	h	s	a	s	a	g
t	m	t	x	o	a	f	b	s	t
s	o	s	l	r	o	i	c	i	r

What is sung during Christmas time?

_____

- -

_____

Name _____   **Date** _____

Find the Tree

Directions: Help the star find the Christmas tree.

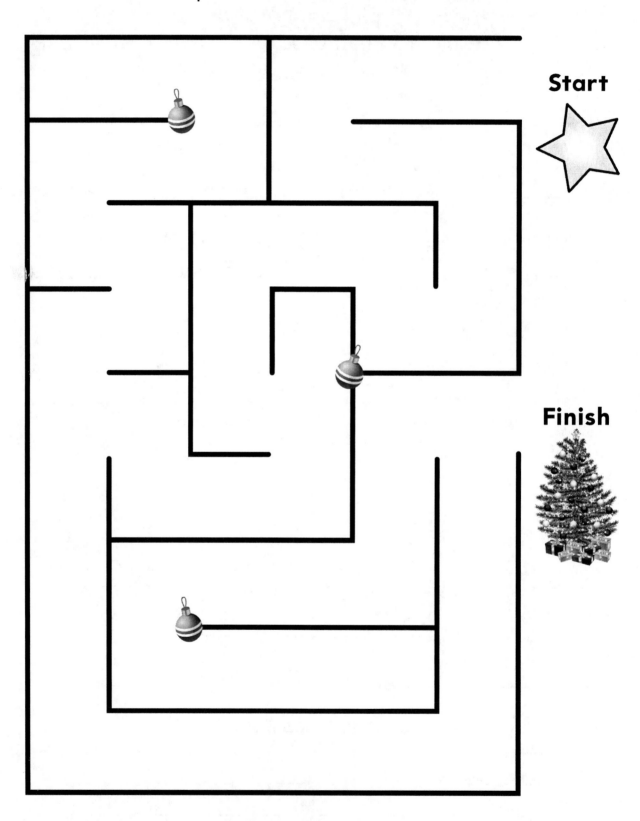

Connect the Ornaments

Directions: Match each addition problem on the left to its answer on the right.

 4 + 4 =

 10

2 + 8 =

 12

9 + 3 =

 8

 5 + 4 =

 4

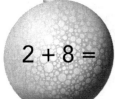 2 + 2 =

 9

Name _____ Date _____

Christmas Then and Now

Directions: Give each student one line to read. Have everyone read the last line together.

Reader 1:   Baby Jesus was born

Reader 2:   To Mary and Joseph on one cold morn.

Reader 3:   His very first bed was chock full of hay.

Reader 4:   But this was our very first Christmas Day!

Reader 5:   The shepherds came, and even some kings.

Reader 6:   They brought some gifts, some special things.

Reader 7:   We tell stories of Santa with gifts in his sleigh.

Reader 8:   We cannot wait until he's on his way.

Reader 9:   We put up a tree with lots of bright lights.

Reader 10: We count off the days and count off the nights.

Reader 11: Some people say it's the best time of the year.

Reader 12: More people are kind. They're full of good cheer.

Reader 13: The lessons of Christmas are good any day.

Reader 14: Let's hope the good feelings never go away.

Reader 15: So everybody, we want to say,

Everyone: Have a very merry Christmas day!

Handprint Christmas Tree

Directions: Make a tree for the winter holidays.

Materials

- *Christmas Template* (page 252)
- construction paper (red, green, brown, and yellow)
- pencil
- scissors and glue
- tree decorations (glitter, ribbon, etc.)

Steps

1. Trace five hands onto green construction paper.
2. Cut out the handprints. Curl up the fingers a bit.
3. Cut out the star and trunk from the *Christmas Template*.
4. Trace and cut out a trunk from the brown construction paper. Place it at the bottom.
5. Put two hand cutouts across the paper to make the widest part of the tree. Glue them down.
6. Glue the next two hand cutouts just above. Then top the tree with the last hand cutout.
7. Trace and cut out a star from yellow paper. Glue it at the top of the tree.
8. Decorate the tree with items such as glitter and ribbon.

Christmas Template

Ramadan
Ninth Month of the Islamic Calendar

Background Information

More than one billion Muslims around the world observe Ramadan for a month each year. There are five pillars of the Muslim faith, each significant during Ramadan. *Shahada* (shah-HAH-duh), or testimony of faith, is considered to be the most important. The second pillar, *Salat* (suh-LAHT), encompasses five periods of prayer during the day: dawn, noon, midafternoon, sunset, and night. The third pillar is *Zakat* (zuh-KAHT), which is alms giving or charity. They believe that generosity and charity during this time earns rewards in plentitude.

The fourth pillar is fasting, *Saum* (SOHM), between the hours of sunrise and sunset. This teaches self-discipline and reminds the faithful that they are blessed with plenty. People abstain not only from food but they also abstain from bad habits. Some people, such as senior citizens, children, and pregnant women, are exempt from fasting. The final pillar, *Hajj* (HAJ), is a form of pilgrimage. More than two million Muslims will travel to the holy city of Mecca for the pilgrimage. Muslims are urged to complete this pilgrimage at least once in their lifetimes.

The exact timing of this special religious month changes every year. The entire cycle takes 35 years to complete. Because a key element of the month is fasting between sunrise and sunset, the length of the fasting day will vary depending on the time of the year and a person's country. The average Ramadan day is about $13\frac{1}{2}$ hours. The day of fasting is broken after sunset with prayers and the eating of three dates. Meals are often special throughout the month, with family and friends breaking the fast together.

After dinner, Muslims may go to mosques to continue their worship. The 27th night is especially important. Called the *Night of Power* or *Night of Destiny,* it is believed that the prophet Muhammad received the first revelation of the holy book, the *Qur'an* (koo-RAHN). Muslims are encouraged to read part or all of the Qur'an during the month of Ramadan. In many mosques, $\frac{1}{30}$ of the Qur'an is read each night. The end of Ramadan is celebrated with a joyous festival, *Eid Al-Fitr,* the Festival of Breaking the Fast.

Recommended Books

Addasi, Maha. 2008. *The White Nights of Ramadan.* Honesdale, PA: Boyds Mill Press.

Douglass, Susan L. 2004. *Ramadan.* Minneapolis, MN: Carolrhoda.

Name _____ **Date** _____

Ramadan Riddles

Directions: Use the Word Bank to solve the Ramadan riddles below.

Word Bank

card   family   moon   money

---

1. People might give this on the last day of Ramadan.

What is it?

____ ____ ____ ____

- - - - - - - - - - - - - - - - - -

____ ____ ____ ____

2. Ramadan starts in the ninth month. Each month is based on this.

What is it?

____ ____ ____ ____

- - - - - - - - - - - - - - - - - -

____ ____ ____ ____

3. People share this with the poor during Ramadan.

What is it?

____ ____ ____ ____ ____

- - - - - - - - - - - - - - - - - -

____ ____ ____ ____ ____

Name _____ Date _____

Do Your Best

Directions: Use the Word Bank to unscramble the good deeds below.

Word Bank

be kind   share   study hard

be truthful   pick up trash

---

1. eb   nikd

_____

- -

_____

2. rheas

_____

- -

_____

3. kcip   pu   shrat

_____

- -

_____

4. eb   ttruhluf

_____

- -

_____

5. dusty   darh

_____

- -

Name _____ **Date** _____

Connect the Suns

Directions: Match each addition problem on the left to its answer on the right.

 12 + 2 =

 12

 4 + 8 =

 14

 11 + 5 =

 11

 10 + 1 =

 16

7 + 3 =

 10

Flags of the Middle East

Directions: Follow the directions to color each Middle Eastern flag below.

United Arab Emirates Flag

- Color the bottom stripe black.
- Color the top stripe green.

- Leave the middle stripe white.
- Color the left stripe red.

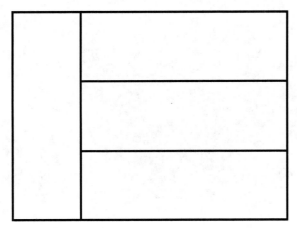

Yemen Flag

- Color the top stripe red.
- Leave the middle stripe white.

- Color the bottom stripe black.

Name _____ **Date** _____

Look Again Ramadan!

Directions: These pictures look a lot alike. Circle the 5 differences on the picture on the bottom.

Name _____ **Date** _____

The Month of Ramadan

Directions: Give each student one line to learn. Have everyone read the last verse together.

Reader 1: Ramadan is here!

Reader 2: The moon is new.

Reader 3: Ramadan is here!

Reader 4: This is what you do:

Reader 5: Be kind to each other.

Reader 6: Share what you can.

Reader 7: Help those who are poor.

Reader 8: That's a good plan.

Reader 9: Read from the Qur'an.

Reader 10: It says what to do.

Reader 11: Be a better person

Reader 12: All the year through.

Reader 13: Ramadan is here.

Reader 14: It's a very fine way.

Reader 15: To learn to be better

Everyone: With each passing day.

Ramadan Moon

Directions: The moon is very special during Ramadan. Make a sky picture just for Ramadan.

Materials

- *Ramadan Template* (page 261)

- black or dark blue construction paper

- white construction paper

- pencil

- scissors

- glue

Steps

1. Cut out and trace several stars and moons from the *Ramadan Template* onto the white construction paper. Cut them out.

2. Place the stars and moons on the black or dark blue construction paper.

3. When you are happy with how it looks, glue them in place.

Stars and Moons Template

Birthdays

Background Information

The Bible discusses a celebration held by King Pharaoh on his birthday, perhaps the first birthday party in written records. For many years, although people around the world celebrated the birth or naming of a child, kings or the elite were the only people thought to be important enough to warrant a party. Over time, people of more humble means adopted the practice of holding a celebration.

In ancient times, people believed that a person was vulnerable to harm, brought by bad spirits, on one's birthday. Family and friends gathered with gifts and noisemakers to ward off the spirits. Candles were lit to send messages or prayers to the gods. The Greeks created the birthday cake and adorned it with candles in honor of the moon goddess, Artemis. Birthday balloons date back to the creation of a ball-like toy from animal bladders or intestines filled with water or air. Jesters in Europe entertained with them. Although greeting cards have been used by some cultures for thousands of years, the sending of birthday cards probably originated in England in the early 1900s.

Around the World

Africa: Children are officially brought into the community through a ceremony.

Australia: People have barbecues and eat fairy bread, a soft white bread, with butter and colored sprinkles.

China: On a child's first birthday, he or she is placed in the center of objects such as coins, a doll, or a book. Whatever the baby reaches for predicts the future. Long noodles are eaten for a long life.

England: Trinkets are baked inside a cake. The trinket that is in the honoree's slice predicts the future for the person.

India: Children wear colorful clothes to school and pass out chocolates.

Korea: Families have a feast on the 100th day following a child's birth.

Mexico: Piñatas are filled with treats and broken open.

Russia: People celebrate with a birthday pie.

Recommended Books

Carle, Eric. 1986. *The Secret Birthday Message*. New York: HarperCollins.

Forrester, Tina and Sheryl Shapiro. 2003. *The Birthday Book*. Vancouver, CN: Annick Press.

Rey, Margaret and H. A. Rey. 2003. *Curious George and the Birthday Surprise*. New York: Houghton Mifflin.

Name _____ Date _____

Birthday Riddles

Directions: Use the Word Bank to solve the Birthday riddles below.

Word Bank

cake	candles	cards	king

1.  The first birthday parties were for rulers.

What kind is this one?

_____ _____ _____ _____

- - - - - - - - - - - - - - - - - -

_____ _____ _____ _____

2.  The Greeks made the first one. It was for the moon goddess.

What is it?

_____ _____ _____ _____

- - - - - - - - - - - - - - - - - -

_____ _____ _____ _____

3.   People put these on a cake.

What are they?

_____ _____ _____ _____ _____ _____ _____

- -

_____ _____ _____ _____ _____ _____ _____

Name _____   Date _____

Mixed-Up Birthdays

Directions: Use the Word Bank to unscramble the birthday words below.

Word Bank

balloons   bows   cake   piñata

1. **llabonos**

   _____

2. **wsob**

   _____

3. **kaec**

   _____

4. **ñpiata**

   _____

Name _____   **Date** _____

Connect the Candles

Directions: Cut out the candle parts below. Glue the candlesticks to a sheet of construction paper. Then glue each flame above the candlestick that answers the subtraction problem.

Finish the Menu

Directions: These things might be eaten at a birthday party. Fill in the missing letters to finish each word.

1.

    ___ ___
    - - - - -   - - - - -
    c ___ pc ___ ke

2.

    ___ ___
    - - - - -   - - - - -
    ___ i z z ___

3.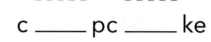

    ___ ___
    - - - - -   - - - - -
    h ___ t   d ___ g

4.

    ___ ___
    - - - - -   - - - - -
    ___ t r a w ___ e r r i e s

5.

    ___
    - - - - -
    ___ p p l e s

6.

    ___ ___
    - - - - -   - - - - -
    ___ c e   c r e a ___

#51046—The Big Book of Holidays and Cultural Celebrations

Name _____ **Date** _____

Birthday Poem

Directions: Make an acrostic poem for a birthday. Write a word or phrase for each letter of the word *birthday*.

B _____

_____

I _____

_____

R _____

_____

T _____

_____

H _____

_____

D _____

_____

A _____

_____

Y _____

_____

Make a Cake

Directions: Make your own birthday cake. Fill out the details below. Then draw your cake.

_____

• Flavor of cake _____

• Shape _____

• Number of layers _____

• Color of main frosting _____

• Number of candles _____

Draw your cake here. Then color it. Don't forget the candles!

Happy Birthday Cards

Directions: Make a birthday card for someone special.

Materials

- *Candle Template* (page 270)

- construction paper

- variety of patterned paper (e.g., wrapping paper)

- scissors

- glue

- gold glitter

- marker

Birthday Message Examples

Happy Birthday!

Have a great birthday!

Make it a great day!

Steps

1. Cut out and trace the candles from the *Candle Template* onto patterned paper.

2. Fold the construction paper in half. Arrange and glue the candles on the front cover. They can be in a straight row or at different heights.

3. Place glue in the flames. Sprinkle gold glitter onto the glue.

4. Write a message inside the card. Sign your name.

5. Share your card with someone special.

Candle Template

#51046—*The Big Book of Holidays and Cultural Celebrations*

New Year's Day

New Year Riddles (page 9)

1. party hat

2. calendar

3. midnight

Drop That Ball (page 10)

1. soccer

2. bowling

3. beach

Connect the Party Hats (page 11)

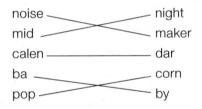

4 + 3 = 9
2 + 7 = 7
10 + 5 = 15
8 + 4 = 11
9 + 2 = 12

Connect the New Year's Words (page 12)

noise — night
mid — maker
calen — dar
ba — corn
pop — by

My New Year's Resolutions (pages 13–14)

Answers will vary.

Martin Luther King Jr. Day

Dr. King Riddles (page 18)

1. church

2. bus

3. peace

Words of Peace (page 19)

1. friends

2. dream

3. dove

4. hands

Connect the Dr. King Words (page 20)

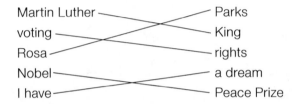

Martin Luther — Parks
voting — King
Rosa — rights
Nobel — a dream
I have — Peace Prize

Dr. King Word Search (page 21)

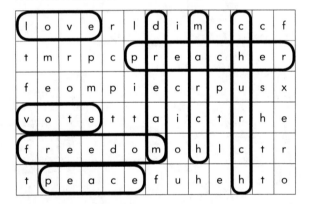

Connect the Doves (page 22)

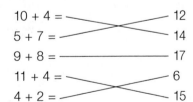

10 + 4 = 12
5 + 7 = 14
9 + 8 = 17
11 + 4 = 6
4 + 2 = 15

"I Have a Dream" Poem (page 23)

Answers will vary.

Chinese New Year

Chinese New Year Riddles (page 26)

1. dragon
2. lantern
3. tiger

Chinese Zodiac Animals (page 27)

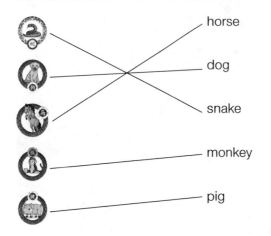

horse

dog

snake

monkey

pig

Connect the Parade Words (page 28)

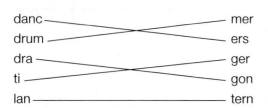

danc — mer
drum — ers
dra — ger
ti — gon
lan — tern

Follow the Zodiac Animal! (page 29)

Start

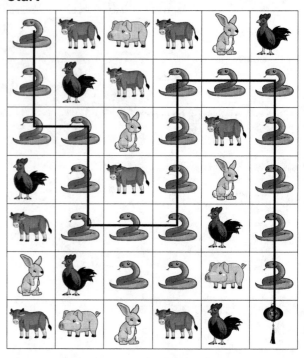

Zodiac Search (page 30)

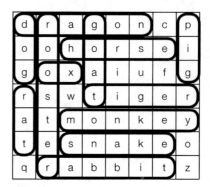

d	r	a	g	o	n	c	p
o	o	h	o	r	s	e	i
g	o	x	a	i	u	f	g
r	s	w	t	i	g	e	r
a	t	m	o	n	k	e	y
t	e	s	n	a	k	e	o
q	r	a	b	b	i	t	z

Groundhog Day

Groundhog Day Riddles (page 35)

1. veggies
2. winter
3. spring

How's the Weather? (page 36)

1. cloudy

2. hot

3. rainy

4. windy

Connect the Groundhogs (page 37)

12 – 4 =	7
10 – 3 =	3
5 – 2 =	8
9 – 5 =	9
11 – 2 =	4

Connect the Weather Words (page 38)

snow	drop
rain	shine
sun	flake
spring	time
um	brella

Winter or Spring? Chart (page 40)

The order of the answers will vary.

Winter	Spring

Lincoln's Birthday

Abraham Lincoln Riddles (page 45)

1. cabin

2. reading

3. hat

Connect the Hats (page 46)

10 – 2 =	4
4 – 3 =	8
8 – 4 =	1
9 – 3 =	0
5 – 5 =	6

Look Again Lincoln! (page 47)

Lincoln Word Search (page 48)

a	b	e	p	f	a	t	h	e	r	s
s	t	o	r	e	o	w	n	e	r	c
o	d	c	e	r	l	m	n	u	i	j
l	o	g	s	p	l	i	t	t	e	r
d	f	g	i	j	k	h	v	d	y	u
i	s	g	d	l	a	w	y	e	r	b
e	x	c	e	f	j	i	o	m	l	p
r	u	b	n	e	s	k	n	o	v	d
p	o	s	t	m	a	s	t	e	r	e

Follow the Penny! (page 49)

Start

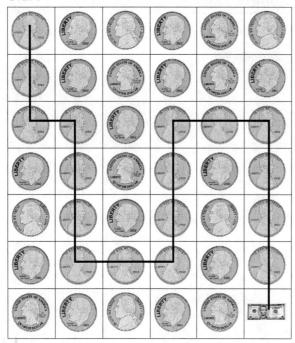

Valentine's Day

Valentine's Day Riddles (page 53)

1. cupid
2. cards
3. roses

Roses for You (page 54)

1. purple
2. pink
3. red
4. orange

Connect the Valentine Words (page 55)

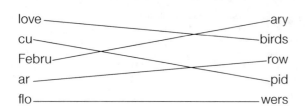

Find Cupid's Heart (page 56)

Connect the Hearts (page 57)

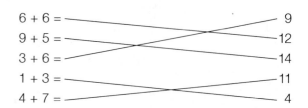

100th Day of School

(pages 61–66)

Answers will vary on all activity pages.

President's Day

George Washington Riddles (page 69)

1. George
2. tree
3. February

Presidents Word Scramble (page 70)

1. First Lady
2. White House
3. Washington
4. Flag

Connect the President Words (page 71)

Capi ——————————— tol
calen ———————— ag
fl ————————— dar
White Hou ——————— se
str ——————————— ipes

The Truth or a Fib? (page 72)

Answers will vary.

Follow the Cherries! (page 73)

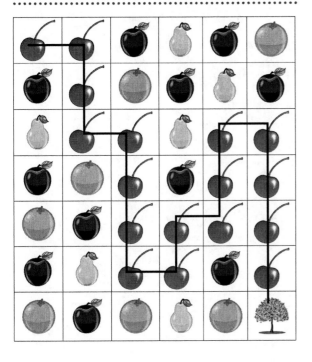

Saint Patrick's Day

Saint Patrick's Day Riddles (page 78)

1. gold
2. rainbow
3. clover

Connect the Clovers (page 79)

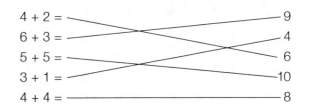

4 + 2 =   9
6 + 3 =   4
5 + 5 =   6
3 + 1 =   10
4 + 4 = ——————————— 8

Pot of Gold! (page 80)

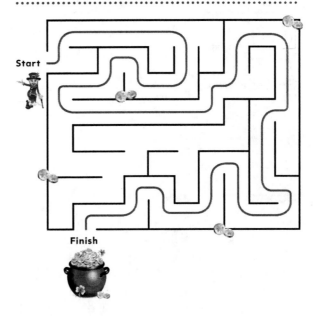

Letters of Gold (page 81)

1. g **o** l d
2. p **o** t
3. s h **o** e s
4. h **a** t
5. s h **a** m r o c k
6. r **a** i n b o w

Follow the Four-Leaf Clovers (page 82)

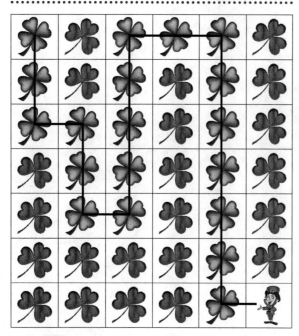

Easter

Easter Riddles (page 87)

1. basket
2. eggs
3. hare

Bunny Word Search (page 88)

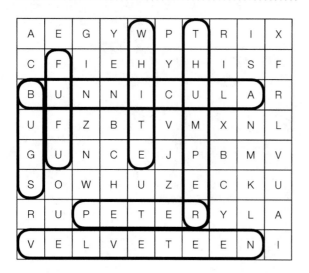

Connect the Eggs (page 89)

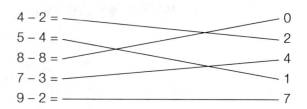

Fill the Easter Basket (page 90)

Hop to It! (page 91)

basket

Passover

Seder Time! (page 96)

1. candles
2. matzo
3. king

Passover Foods! (page 97)

1. matzo
2. parsley
3. celery
4. potato

Connect the Pyramids (page 98)

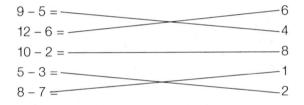

$9 - 5 =$ — 4
$12 - 6 =$ — 6
$10 - 2 =$ — 8
$5 - 3 =$ — 2
$8 - 7 =$ — 1

Crossing the Red Sea (page 99)

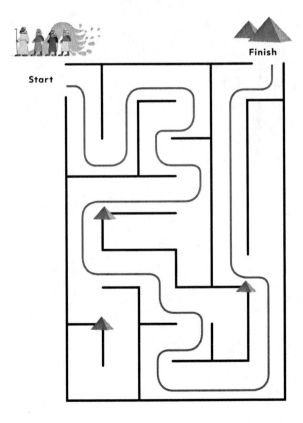

Start

Finish

Look Again Passover! (page 100)

April Fools' Day

April Fools' Riddles (page 104)

1. pig dig
2. big pig
3. hog log

Funny Word Connections (page 105)

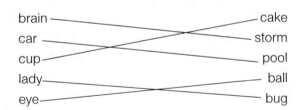

brain — storm
car — pool
cup — cake
lady — bug
eye — ball

Joke Match-Ups (page 106)

What kind of hair do oceans have?	wavy
Why does the flamingo only lift up one leg?	If it lifted up two it would fall over.
What is a volcano?	a mountain with hiccups
What runs but never walks?	water
Why did the clock get sick?	It got run down.
What is a tornado?	mother nature doing the twist
How do you make a milk shake?	Give it a good scare.

April Fools' Search (page 107)

v	l	g	i	g	g	l	e
w	a	i	z	t	q	x	c
s	u	r	p	r	i	s	e
i	g	w	r	i	p	d	f
l	h	y	a	c	r	s	u
l	r	l	n	k	h	r	n
y	s	m	k	o	j	t	n
c	h	u	c	k	l	e	y

Earth Day

Earth Day Riddles (page 112)

1. recycle
2. reuse
3. Earth

Recycle It! (page 113)

1. paper
2. tires
3. cans
4. glasses

Earth Day Word Search (page 114)

b	c	d	e	o	w	p	l	e	a	v	e	s
e	g	g	s	h	e	l	l	s	j	k	l	g
c	o	f	f	e	e	g	r	o	u	n	d	s
r	t	o	t	j	d	l	g	r	u	f	p	t
c	y	u	n	k	s	f	r	e	j	q	j	r
d	n	l	n	o	g	v	a	c	m	s	m	a
v	g	t	p	e	e	l	s	v	n	z	g	w
x	t	e	a	b	a	g	s	x	g	a	n	b

Earth Day—Clean Day (page 115)

Connect the Earths (page 117)

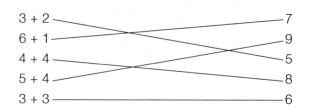

3 + 2   7
6 + 1   9
4 + 4   5
5 + 4   8
3 + 3   6

May Day

May Day Riddles (page 120)

1. flowers
2. basket
3. queen

Funny Flower Fun! (page 121)

1. butterfly bush
2. buttons
3. dragon tail

Find the Maypole (page 122)

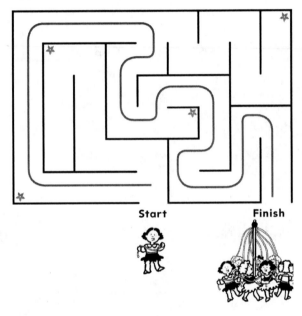

Start   Finish

May Day Jokes (page 123)

What flowers are on your face?	tulips
What is a bee's favorite flower?	honeysuckle
What kind of plant did the dishwasher use?	bottlebrush
What is a frog's favorite flower?	crocus
Why couldn't the flower ride a bike?	It had no petals.
How is the letter A like a flower?	Both are followed by bees.

Maypole Puzzle (page 124)

1. lime
2. rose
3. silver
4. teal
5. rust
6. ruby
7. lemon

May Day Math (page 125)

$3 + 4 =$ — 4
$2 + 2 =$ — 7
$1 + 7 =$ — 9
$5 + 4 =$ — 8
$6 + 0 =$ — 6

Cinco de Mayo

Cinco de Mayo Riddles (page 129)

1. Mexico
2. flag
3. fiesta

Spanish and English (page 130)

		English	Spanish
1.		rose	rosa
2.		bank	banco
3.		band	banda
4.		jar	jarra

Look Again Cinco de Mayo! (page 131)

Fiesta Food Fun (page 133)

1. taco
2. limes
3. grapes
4. pear
5. peach

Connect the Maracas (page 134)

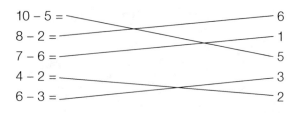

10 – 5 =   6
8 – 2 =   1
7 – 6 =   5
4 – 2 =   3
6 – 3 =   2

Mother's Day

Ways to Say Mom (page 138)

1. mom
2. mother
3. mommy
4. mama
5. ma
6. mum

Animal Moms (page 139)

1. elephant
2. koala
3. alligator

Mother Palindrome Fun (page 140)

1. mom
2. pop
3. eye
4. tot
5. Bob
6. bib

Find the Mother (page 142)

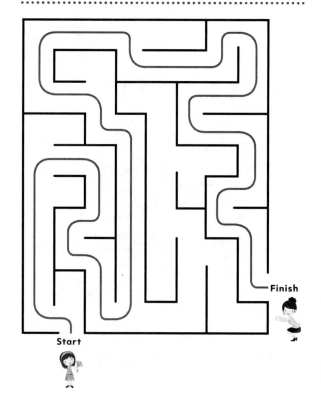

Memorial Day

Memorial Day Riddles (page 146)

1. flag

2. grave

3. May

Memorial Day Words (page 147)

1. jeep

2. eagle

3. medal

4. grave

Memorial Day Line Up! (page 148)

1. band

2. drummers

3. floats

4. Girl Scouts

5. soldiers

6. veterans

Connect the Medals (page 149)

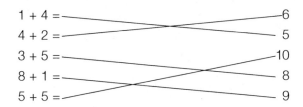

$1 + 4 =$ — 6
$4 + 2 =$ — 5
$3 + 5 =$ — 10
$8 + 1 =$ — 8
$5 + 5 =$ — 9

Memorial Day Search (page 150)

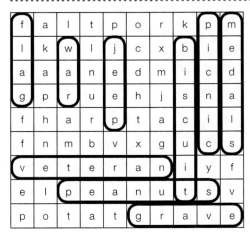

Follow the Eagles! (page 151)

Start

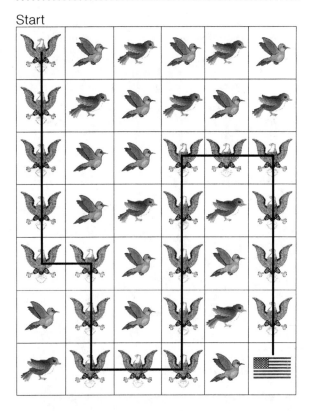

Father's Day

Ways to Say Dad (page 155)

1. dad

2. father

3. daddy

4. dada

5. pop

6. papa

Animal Dads (page 156)

1. lion

2. frog

3. penguin

Father's Day Search (page 158)

p	o	d	a	n	a	d	a	t	e	s
g	r	a	n	d	f	a	t	h	e	r
m	o	d	p	o	a	d	k	a	l	m
p	o	p	p	a	t	d	d	i	d	n
o	s	t	a	f	h	y	o	y	t	b
p	u	v	p	d	e	e	u	m	v	l
c	i	l	a	d	r	d	a	f	h	e

Connect the Ties (page 159)

10 – 2 = ———— 4
11 – 1 = ———— 10
8 – 4 = ———— 8
5 – 2 = ———— 5
9 – 4 = ———— 3

Independence Day

Independence Day Riddles (page 163)

1. July 4
2. flag
3. tea

Birthday of a Nation Words (page 164)

1. picnic
2. fireworks
3. parade
4. sparklers
5. concert

Connect the Flags (page 165)

7 – 3 = ———— 2
8 – 6 = ———— 4
10 – 5 = ———— 0
9 – 8 = ———— 5
4 – 4 = ———— 1

Stars in Our Flag (page 166)

1. 4
2. 13
3. 12
4. 9
5. 7
6. 15

Find the Flag (page 167)

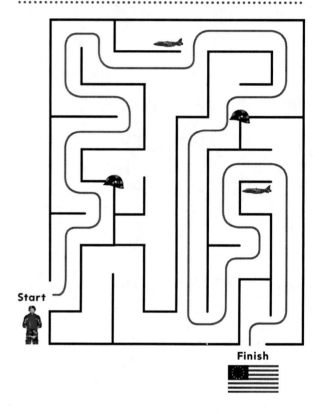

Start

Finish

Labor Day

Helpful Workers (page 171)

1. chef
2. farmer
3. doctor

Animals at Work (page 172)

1. dog
2. mule
3. horse
4. pig

Connect the Leaves (page 173)

4 + 2 = ———— 4
5 + 4 = ———— 6
3 + 1 = ———— 9
7 + 3 = ———— 8
6 + 2 = ———— 10

Connect the Workers and Tools (page 174)

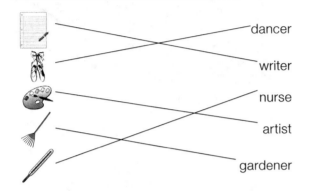

dancer

writer

nurse

artist

gardener

Labor Day Line Up! (page 175)

1. builders
2. cooks
3. mailmen
4. nurses
5. pilots
6. trainers

Look Again Labor Day! (page 176)

Rosh Hashanah and Yom Kippur

Rosh Hashanah and Yom Kippur Riddles (page 180)

1. apple
2. shofar
3. pray

Yom Kippur Mixed-Up Words (page 181)

1. candles
2. pray
3. sing
4. cake

Connect the Rosh Hashanah and Yom Kippur Words (page 182)

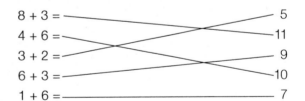

sho ———————— far
can ———————— dles
read ———————— ey
hon ———————— ing
ap ———————— ple

Yom Kippur Message (page 183)

This is the day to forgive.

Connect the Shofars (page 184)

8 + 3 = ———— 5
4 + 6 = ———— 11
3 + 2 = ———— 9
6 + 3 = ———— 10
1 + 6 = ———— 7

Look Again Rosh Hashanah! (page 185)

Look Again Columbus Day! (page 190)

Columbus Day

Columbus Day Riddles (page 188)

1. ship

2. Spain

3. ocean

Sailing Away! (page 189)

1. clouds

2. bird

3. ship

4. sun

Help Columbus! (page 192)

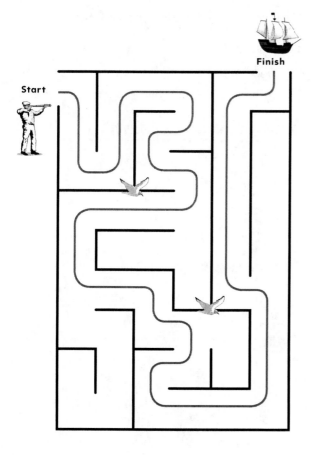

Animals in India Word Search (page 198)

r	h	i	n	o	c	e	r	o	s
h	c	e	s	v	a	l	x	s	v
a	n	t	e	a	t	e	r	o	n
y	t	i	r	w	e	p	v	l	k
d	s	g	s	c	f	h	b	m	l
f	g	e	m	a	c	a	q	u	e
w	e	r	i	u	a	n	r	x	b
x	z	b	e	d	s	t	y	d	s
f	l	y	i	n	g	f	o	x	f
e	l	e	o	p	a	r	d	b	s

Find the Wealth (page 199)

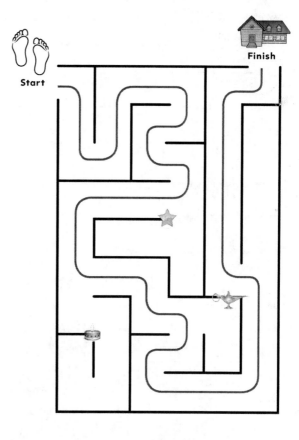

Diwali

Diwali Riddles (page 196)

1. clothes

2. gifts

3. clean

Diwali Fun (page 197)

1. diya

2. candle

3. star

4. lamp

Connect the Oil Lamps (page 200)

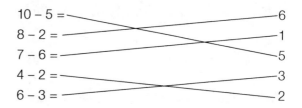

```
10 – 5 =                    6
8 – 2 =                     1
7 – 6 =                     5
4 – 2 =                     3
6 – 3 =                     2
```

Halloween and Day of the Dead

Halloween Fun! (page 204)

1. black cat
2. ghost
3. mask

Mixed-Up Halloween Words (page 205)

1. ghost
2. cat
3. spider
4. bat

Connect the Halloween Costumes (page 206)

astro————————————naut
lady————————————on
drag————————————bug
qu—————————————bot
ro—————————————een

Halloween Safety (page 207)

Have fun, but stay safe.

Follow the Grinning Jack-o'-Lanterns! (page 208)

Start

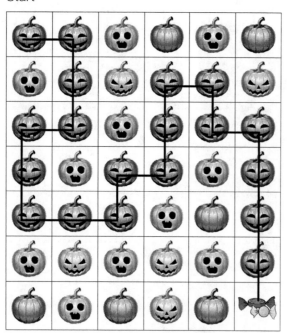

Veterans Day

Veterans Day Riddles (page 212)

1. tank
2. jeep
3. jet

Getting Dressed (page 213)

1. shirt
2. socks
3. boots
4. helmet

At Your Service (page 214)

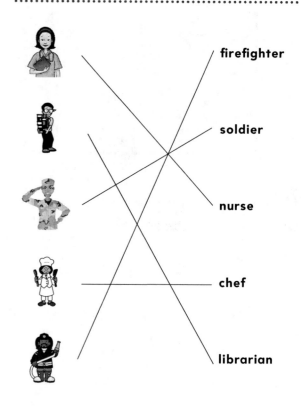

firefighter

soldier

nurse

chef

librarian

Look Again Veterans Day! (page 215)

Follow the Camouflage! (page 216)

Start

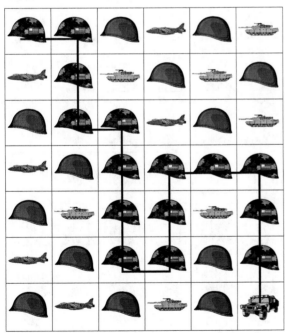

Thanksgiving

Thanksgiving Riddles (page 220)

1. fish
2. Pilgrims
3. corn

The Menu (page 221)

1. duck
2. fish
3. corn
4. grapes

Connect the Feast (page 222)

tur ———————— tato
cran ——————— key
sweet po ———— berries
pump ————————— kin

Dressing as a Pilgrim (page 223)

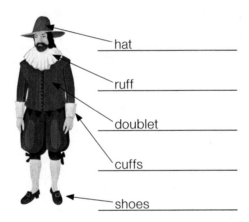

hat

ruff

doublet

cuffs

shoes

Hanukkah

Hanukkah Riddles (page 228)

1. latkes
2. olives
3. dreidel

Hanukkah Lights (page 229)

1. moon
2. candle
3. star
4. sun

Connect the Dreidels (page 230)

$3 + 3 =$ ⎯⎯⎯⎯⎯⎯ 9
$4 + 5 =$ ⎯⎯⎯⎯⎯⎯ 6
$8 + 2 =$ ⎯⎯⎯⎯⎯⎯ 7
$2 + 5 =$ ⎯⎯⎯⎯⎯⎯ 10
$1 + 3 =$ ⎯⎯⎯⎯⎯⎯ 4

Eight Days of Hanukkah (page 231)

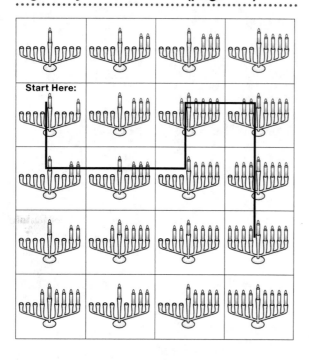

Hanukkah Line Up! (page 233)

1. candles
2. dreidel
3. lamp
4. latkes
5. moon
6. sun

Kwanzaa

Kwanzaa Riddles (page 237)

1. cup
2. gifts
3. mat

First Fruits (page 238)

1. orange
2. grapes
3. pear
4. corn

Connect the Kwanzaa Words (page 239)

kin ⎯⎯⎯⎯⎯⎯ dles
uni ⎯⎯⎯⎯⎯⎯ ara
can ⎯⎯⎯⎯⎯⎯ ty cup
corn ⎯⎯⎯⎯⎯⎯ stalk
ap ⎯⎯⎯⎯⎯⎯ ples

Connect the Kinaras (page 240)

Start

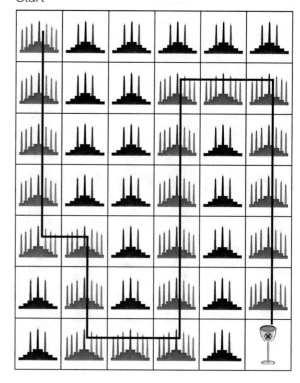

Kwanzaa Harvest (page 241)

Fruit	apples
Vegetables	carrots
Grains	wheat
Meats	bacon

Find the Kinara (page 242)

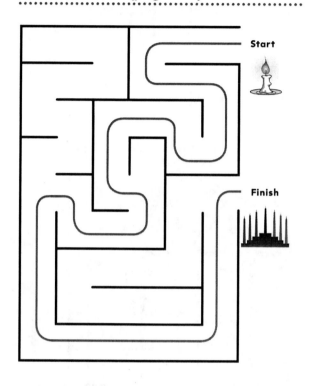

Christmas

Christmas Riddles (page 245)

1. Santa

2. carols

3. elves

Decorate the Tree! (page 246)

1. angel

2. star

3. balls

4. lights

Get to Work! (page 247)

Start	a	c	e	i	ⓒ	p	u	f	ⓐ
c	k	r	ⓢ	h	s	a	s	a	g
t	m	t	x	o	a	f	b	s	t
s	o	s	①	r	ⓞ	i	c	i	ⓡ

carols

Find the Tree (page 248)

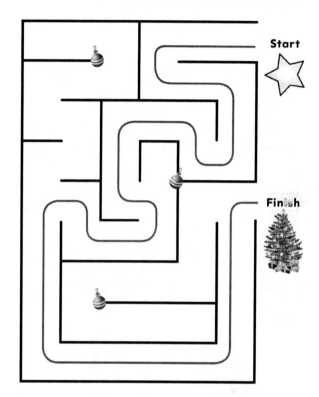

Connect the Ornaments (page 249)

```
4 + 4 =                     10
2 + 8 =                     12
9 + 3 =                      8
5 + 4 =                      4
2 + 2 =                      9
```

Ramadan

Ramadan Riddles (page 254)

1. card
2. moon
3. money

Do Your Best (page 255)

1. be kind
2. share
3. pick up trash
4. be truthful
5. study hard

Connect the Suns (page 256)

$12 + 2 =$ 12
$4 + 8 =$ 14
$11 + 5 =$ 11
$10 + 1 =$ 16
$7 + 3 =$ 10

Look Again Ramadan! (page 258)

Birthdays

Birthday Riddles (page 263)

1. king
2. cake
3. candles

Mixed-Up Birthdays (page 264)

1. balloons
2. bows
3. cake
4. piñata

Connect the Candles (page 265)

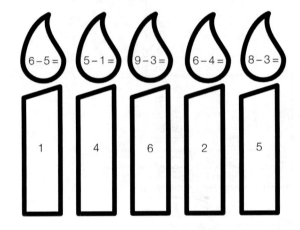

Finish the Menu (page 266)

1. c u p c a k e
2. p i z z a
3. h o t   d o g
4. s t r a w b e r r i e s
5. a p p l e s
6. i c e   c r e a m

Contents of the Digital Resource CD

Teacher Background Information Pages		
Pages	**Title**	**Filename**
8–16	New Year's Day Unit	newyearsdayunit.pdf
17–24	Martin Luther King Jr. Day Unit	martinlutherkingjrunit.pdf
25–33	Chinese New Year Unit	chinesenewyearunit.pdf
34–43	Groundhog Day Unit	groundhogunit.pdf
44–51	Lincoln's Birthday Unit	lincolnsbirthdayunit.pdf
52–59	Valentine's Day Unit	valentinesdayunit.pdf
60–67	100th Day of School Unit	100thdayunit.pdf
68–76	Presidents' Day Unit	presidentsdayunit.pdf
77–85	Saint Patrick's Day Unit	saintpatricksdayunit.pdf
86–94	Easter Unit	easterunit.pdf
95–102	Passover Unit	passoverunit.pdf
103–110	April Fools' Day Unit	aprilfoolsdayunit.pdf
111–118	Earth Day Unit	earthdayunit.pdf
119–127	May Day Unit	maydayunit.pdf
128–136	Cinco de Mayo Unit	cincodemayounit.pdf
137–144	Mother's Day Unit	mothersdayunit.pdf
145–153	Memorial Day Unit	memorialdayunit.pdf
154–161	Father's Day Unit	fathersdayunit.pdf
162–169	Independence Day Unit	independencedayunit.pdf
170–178	Labor Day Unit	labordayunit.pdf
179–186	Rosh Hashanah/Yom Kippur Unit	roshhashanah_yomkippurunit.pdf
187–194	Columbus Day Unit	columbusdayunit.pdf
195–202	Diwali Unit	diwaliunit.pdf
203–210	Halloween/Day of the Dead Unit	halloween_dayofdeadunit.pdf
211–218	Veterans Day Unit	veteransdayunit.pdf
219–226	Thanksgiving Unit	thanksgivingunit.pdf
227–235	Hanukkah Unit	hanukkahunit.pdf
236–243	Kwanzaa Unit	kwanzaaunit.pdf
244–252	Christmas Unit	christmasunit.pdf
253–261	Ramadan Unit	ramadanunit.pdf
262–270	Birthdays Unit	birthdaysunit.pdf

Page	**Teacher Resources**	**Folder Name**
N/A	Craft Pictures	Craft Pictures

Notes

Notes

Notes

#51046—The Big Book of Holidays and Cultural Celebrations

© Shell Education